中国思想文化术语多语种对外翻译
标准化建设项目成果
CHINESE THINKING AND CULTURE
MULTILINGUAL TERMINOLOGY DATABASE

中华源·河南故事
CHINESE CIVILIZATION
Stories from Henan

黄河文化
THE YELLOW RIVER CULTURE

主编 刘炯天
EDITOR-IN-CHIEF: LIU JIONGTIAN

河南大学出版社
HENAN UNIVERSITY PRESS
·郑州·

图书在版编目（CIP）数据

中华源·河南故事 . 黄河文化：汉英对照 / 刘炯天主编 . -- 郑州：河南大学出版社，2021.4
　ISBN 978-7-5649-4548-0

Ⅰ . ①中… Ⅱ . ①刘… Ⅲ . ①地方文化 - 河南 - 通俗读物 - 汉、英②黄河流域 - 文化史 - 通俗读物 - 汉、英 Ⅳ . ① G127.61-49 ② K292-49

中国版本图书馆 CIP 数据核字（2021）第 023687 号

责任编辑	阮林耍
责任校对	林方丽
封面设计	翟淼淼
出版发行	河南大学出版社
	地址：郑州市郑东新区商务外环中华大厦2401号　邮编：450046
	电话：0371-86059701（营销部）
	0371-86059750（高等教育与职业教育分公司）
	网址：hupress.henu.edu.cn
排　　版	河南大学出版社设计排版部
印　　刷	河南博雅彩印有限公司
版　　次	2021年4月第1版
印　　次	2021年4月第1次印刷
开　　本	710 mm×1010 mm　1/16
印　　张	13
字　　数	208千
定　　价	65.00元

版权所有，侵权必究
本书如有印装质量问题，请与河南大学出版社营销部联系调换。

"中华源·河南故事"系列丛书编委会

顾　　问	黄友义　杨　平　范大祺
名誉主任	穆为民　何金平　刘炯天
主　　任	付　静
副 主 任	陈　岩　陈志伟　刁玉华　方启雄　介晓磊
	孔留安　李冰冰　李向前　李　镇　梁留科
	刘金锋　牛卫国　屈鹏飞　史永庆　田　凯
	万正峰　王建修　王清义　王自文　许二平
	杨建伟　杨玮斌　张改平　张俊峰　张明超
	张松文　赵卫东

主　　编	付　静
副 主 编	李冰冰
编　　委	陈　玮　丁　锐　高　阳　徐恒振　郑延保

中华源·河南故事·黄河文化

主　　编	刘炯天
副 主 编	左其亭　钱建成（英文）
中文撰稿	陈隆文　梁允华　王　琳　张　伟
英文译者	李晓静　张庆彬　陈行洁　沈　杨
英文审校	〔美〕Rex Troumbley

The Editorial Committee
Chinese Civilization
Stories from Henan

Consultants	Huang Youyi Yang Ping Fan Daqi
Honorary Directors	Mu Weimin He Jinping Liu Jiongtian
Director	Fu Jing
Deputy Directors	Chen Yan Chen Zhiwei Diao Yuhua Fang Qixiong
	Jie Xiaolei Kong Liu'an Li Bingbing Li Xiangqian
	Li Zhen Liang Liuke Liu Jinfeng Niu Weiguo
	Qu Pengfei Shi Yongqing Tian Kai Wan Zhengfeng
	Wang Jianxiu Wang Qingyi Wang Ziwen Xu Erping
	Yang Jianwei Yang Weibin Zhang Gaiping
	Zhang Junfeng Zhang Mingchao Zhang Songwen
	Zhao Weidong
Chief Editor	Fu Jing
Deputy Chief Editor	Li Bingbing
Editors	Chen Wei Ding Rui Gao Yang Xu Hengzhen
	Zheng Yanbao

Chinese Civilization
Stories from Henan
The Yellow River Culture

Editor-in-Chief	Liu Jiongtian
Associate Editors-in-Chief	Zuo Qiting Qian Jiancheng (English Text)
Writers	Chen Longwen Liang Yunhua Wang Lin
	Zhang Wei
Translators	Li Xiaojing Zhang Qingbin Chen Xingjie
	Shen Yang
Translation Proofreader	Rex Troumbley (U. S.)

总　序

　　中国是世界四大文明古国之一，也是世界上唯一的古代文明传统未曾中断的国家。河南省地处中国中东部，是中华文明和中华民族的重要发祥地，在中国五千年的文明史上，河南作为国家政治、经济、文化的中心就长达三千多年。从某种意义上讲，一部河南史就是半部中国史。这里是中华人文始祖黄帝的故乡，是古丝绸之路的东方起点，是少林功夫和陈氏太极的发源地，这里创建了中国历史上最早的都城，镌刻了中国最古老的文字，诞生了中国最初的商业文明。

　　伴随着新时代的荣光，河南经济社会发展迅速，人民生活水平显著提升，这是河南人民自力更生、艰苦奋斗的历史结果，也是对外开放带来的益处。河南经济社会的发展、人民生活方式的改变都植根于深层次的文化积淀。为了让世界更多地了解河南，让河南更好地走向世界，2018年以来，河南省人民政府外事办公室认真研析了这片古老土地上的历史文化资源和时代风貌，组织各领域权威专家学者，编译了"中华源·河南故事"中外文系列丛书，选取黄河文化、河洛文化、老子、庄子、黄帝、少林功夫、太极拳、中医、汉字、丝绸之路、古都、农业、大运河、文物、陶瓷、青铜器、手工艺、书法、杂技、豫菜、豫剧、脱贫攻坚、空中丝绸之路、航空城、南水北调、中国粮谷、红旗渠、焦裕禄等多个主题，力图以故事的方式向世界展现一个立体、全面、真实的河南。

　　当今世界，人类文明无论是在物质还是在精神方面都取得了巨大进步，特别是物质的极大丰富，这在古代世界是完全不能想象的。同时，当代人类也面临着许多突出的难题，比如，贫富差距持续扩大，物欲追求奢华无度，个人主义恶性膨胀，社会诚信不断消减，伦理道德每况愈下，人与自然关系日趋紧张，等等。要解决这些难题，不仅需要运用人类今天的智慧和力量，而且需要运用人类历史上积累和储存的智慧和力量。河南历史文化底蕴深厚、包容性强，在今天仍极具现实意义。中原文化蕴含的思想智慧有助于修身养性，推动人类社会进步发展，焦裕禄精神、红旗渠精神所体现的为民爱民、艰苦奋斗的价值取向是构建人类命运共同体的力量源泉。我们期待与读者们一起从河南故事中汲取更多的智慧和力量，共同创造更加美好的未来。

Series Foreword

China is one of the four ancient civilizations in the world, and is also the only country in the world where the ancient civilization has not been interrupted. Located in east-central China, Henan Province is an important cradle for the Chinese nation and Chinese civilization. In the course of the five thousand years of Chinese history, for more than three thousand years it served as the political, economic and cultural center of the country and therefore, as generally accepted, represents half of the history of China. Henan is the native place of Yellow Emperor, the cradle of Chinese culture, the starting point of the ancient Silk Road in the east, and the birthplace of Shaolin Kungfu and Chen-style Taijiquan—typical examples of the world-renowned Chinese martial arts. It was here that the earliest capital city in China was founded, the oldest Chinese characters engraved, and the earliest commerce took shape.

In the new era, Henan has witnessed rapid growth in its economy and remarkable improvement of people's living conditions owing to the national reform and opening-up policy and unremitting endeavors of the people. Modern economic achievements and social development as well as the changes of way of life could be traced back to its traditional values and cultural heritages. To enable people from other countries to understand Henan, and let the Province integrate more efficiently into the world development, the Foreign Affairs Office of the People's Government of Henan Province has organized teams of authoritative experts and scholars in relevant fields to compile this *Chinese Civilization: Stories from Henan* in Chinese and foreign languages since 2018 by crystallizing the excellence of traditions and outstanding features of modern development. The book series include *The Yellow River Culture*, *Heluo Culture*, *Laozi*, *Zhuangzi*, *The Yellow Emperor*, *Shaolin Kungfu*, *Taijiquan*, *Traditional Chinese Medicine*,

Chinese Characters, *The Silk Road*, *Ancient Chinese Capitals*, *Feeding the People—Agriculture*, *The Grand Canal*, *Cultural Heritage*, *Ceramic*, *Bronze*, *Handicraft Art*, *Calligraphy*, *Acrobatics*, *Henan Cuisine*, *Henan Opera*, *Poverty Alleviation*, *Silk Road in the Air*, *Zhengzhou—An Aviation City*, *South-to-North Water Diversion*, *China Grain Valley*, *Man-Made River—Hongqiqu Canal*, *A Model Official—Jiao Yulu*, etc., presenting a panoramic picture of the Province.

In today's world, human civilization has made great progress in both material accumulation and ethical advancement, and the great abundance of materials today, especially, is beyond the imagination of the ancient people. At the same time, however, modern people are also confronted with a lot of problems, such as the widening gap between the rich and the poor, the indulgence in pursuit of luxury and extravagance, the undesirable extension of individualism, the decline of social integrity, and the increasingly tense relationship between man and nature. To solve the problems, we need to draw on the wisdom and powers developed today as well as those accumulated in the past. Henan is endowed with rich historical and cultural heritages characterized by its inclusiveness, and such heritages remain significant today. The intelligence and wisdom in Henan culture are conducive to self-cultivation and to the promotion of social development. The spirit of serving the people and relentless struggle, as embodied in Jiao Yulu and Man-Made River—Hongqiqu Canal provides source of strength for building a community with a shared future for mankind. It is our hope that wisdom and strength from Henan stories could lead us to a shared brilliant future.

前　言

黄河是中华民族的母亲河。黄河流域以其独特而优越的地理环境，孕育出光辉灿烂的黄河文化，是生生不息、源远流长的中华文明发祥地。斗转星移，岁月流转，以黄河文化为主流的文化，与中国境内的诸多文化互相融合，不断借鉴世界其他文明优秀成果，宛若万流归宗、奔腾入海，形成了丰富多彩、光芒四射的中华民族文化。

黄河文化是中华民族的根魂所系。华夏文明的源头在黄河中下游地区，经过一代代先民的辛勤创造，由涓涓小溪拓展成澎湃奔涌的大河激流，中华文化谱系的连续性、完整性在黄河流域得到最为典型的体现。此外，华夏人文始祖伏羲、黄帝的传说诞生于黄河流域，现代中华姓氏的祖根绝大多数亦发源于此，历代华夏子孙不论迁徙距离有多么遥远、时间有多么久远，对河洛故地、中原故土的记忆始终未曾褪色，成为重要的民族身份象征。黄河文化的根与魂属性是中华民族形成和强大凝聚力产生的源头所在。

黄河文化具有质朴厚重的包容性格。其深深扎根于黄河流域古老的农业文明厚土，宛如层叠深沉的黄土高原，以兼收并蓄的姿态养育出多元丰富的文明成果。从远古时期的裴李岗、龙山、仰韶、二里头文化一脉延伸，经过夏、商、周时期神秘而绚烂的青铜时代，不断吸收、创造，形成秦、汉、隋、唐等大一统帝国耀眼夺目的中原文化，发展为灿若群星、长期领先于世界的物质、精神文明成果。

黄河文化具有与时俱进的创新精神。黄河流域处在东亚农耕文明与游牧文明的交汇地带，以农业为基础的中原文化和以游牧为特色的北方草原文化长期碰撞交流、互相借鉴，形成了黄河文化不断改革调整、适应时代的创新精神，造就了中华文明经久不息的生存活力，演绎了中华民族在不断的挑战中浴火重生、再现繁荣的光辉历程。此外，黄河流域位于古代东、西方交通的核心区域，以丝绸之路为代表的贸易通道，亦成为黄河文明与西方世界文明交流的文化之路，黄河文化得以吸收其他文明优秀的成果，不断融合创新，形成更加多元丰富的文化体系，并对东亚、东南亚的周边国家文化产生持续而深刻的影响。

在近代世界工业革命浪潮涌起之后，以西欧海洋文明为代表的欧洲文化逐渐占据世界舞台的主角地位，中国古老的黄河文化受到严重的冲击和挑战，一度呈现出衰落沉寂的颓靡态势。经过一个多世纪的曲折探索，1949年，中华人民共和国成立之后，在中国共产党的坚强领导下，中国的现代化建设呈现出崭新的风貌，注入近代新鲜血液的黄河文化逐渐焕发出新的生机。如何在实现中华民族伟大复兴目标的过程中，提升以黄河文化为代表的中华文化软实力，造就一个适应新时代要求、充满活力的崭新黄河文化体系，成为新时代中华儿女迫切而重要的现实任务。

我们坚信，具有悠久历史和坚韧生命力的黄河文化，必将在新时代继续凝聚中华民族的强大正能量，推动中国社会的高质量发展；也将会绽放出更加强大的活力，以崭新的姿态屹立于现代世界文明之林！

Preface

The Yellow River is the mother river of the Chinese nation. With its unique geographical environment, the Yellow River Basin, which is the birthplace of the long-standing Chinese civilization, has nurtured the splendid Yellow River culture. Over time, the Yellow River culture, as the mainstream, integrated with many other cultures in China, and kept learning from other civilizations in the world. Just like thousands of streams will eventually merge into a vast ocean, they have gradually grown into the colorful and brilliant Chinese civilization.

The Yellow River culture is the root of the Chinese nation. The source of Chinese civilization is in the middle and lower reaches of the Yellow River. After generations of ancestors' hard work, as the backbone, the Yellow River culture has expanded from gentle streams to turbulent torrents, and typically reflects the continuity and integrity of the Chinese cultural pedigree. In addition, the legends of Fuxi and Yellow Emperor, who are the ancestors of Chinese humanistic culture, originated here, and most ancestral roots of modern Chinese surnames also took here as the source. No matter how long or how far the Chinese people are away from their homeland, the Chinese descendants' memories of the homeland of Heluo and Central Plains have never faded, forming an important symbol of national identities. It's the Yellow River culture, the root and soul of the Chinese people, that holds together our great Chinese nation.

The Yellow River culture is deeply rooted in the ancient agricultural civilization in the Yellow River Basin, so, just like the layered broad Loess Plateau, it is inclusive and eclectic, cultivating diverse and splendid achievements of civilization successfully. Extending from the Peiligang, Longshan, Yangshao, and Erlitou cultures in ancient times, through the mysterious and splendid Bronze Age in Xia, Shang, and Zhou periods, the Yellow River Basin keeps absorbing and creating to establish the splendid Central Plains culture of the unified empires of the Qin, Han, Sui and Tang dynasties. The spectacular culture of the Central

Plains has produced the material and spiritual civilization achievements like brilliant stars, and has led the world over thousands of years.

The Yellow River culture has an innovative spirit of advancing with the times. Since the Yellow River Basin is located at the intersection of East Asian farming civilization and nomadic civilization, the Central Plains culture based on agriculture and the northern grassland culture characterized by nomadism have long sparred, exchanged and learned from each other. This innovative spirit has allowed the Yellow River culture to adapt to the times, and has vigorously driven Chinese civilization forward, demonstrating the Chinese nation's continuing revitalization in the face of constant challenges. The Yellow River Basin lies in the core area of the ancient East—West transportation. The trade channel represented by the Silk Road has also become a cultural road for the exchange between the Yellow River civilization and the Western civilization. The Yellow River culture continuously integrated the best of other civilizations' achievements to establish a more diverse and rich cultural system, producing a lasting and profound impact on the culture of neighboring countries in East Asia and Southeast Asia.

After the wave of Industrial Revolution in the modern world, European culture represented by Western European marine civilization gradually occupied the leading position on the world stage. The ancient Chinese Yellow River culture, which was severely threatened and challenged, once showed a declining and sluggish trend. After more than a century's tortuous exploration, especially after the founding of the People's Republic of China in 1949, China's modernization has taken on a new outlook, and the Yellow River culture, which has been injected with fresh blood from modern times, has gradually shown new vitality. How to enhance the soft power of the Chinese culture represented by the Yellow River culture in the process of achieving the great rejuvenation of the Chinese nation, and create a new vibrant Yellow River cultural system that adapts to the requirements of the new era, has become an urgent and important realistic task for the Chinese people.

We firmly believe that the Yellow River culture, with its distinguished history and tenacious vitality, will continue to marshal the strong positive energy of the Chinese nation and drive the development of Chinese society forward in the new era. It will also bloom with more vitality and stand in the forest of modern world civilizations with a new look!

目 录　　　　　　　　　　　　Contents

第一章　孕育：黄河远上白云间　　　　　　　　　001
　　一、上游：河源高悬云山外　　　　　　　　　006
　　二、中游：郑州桃花峪到河口镇　　　　　　　012
　　三、下游：入海口溯源　　　　　　　　　　　024

Chapter 1　Breed: the Yellow River Coming Far from the White Clouds　　001
　　Ⅰ. The Upstream: High above the Mountains and the Clouds Is the
　　Source of the Yellow River　　　　　　　　　　　　　　　　　　007
　　Ⅱ. The Midstream: from Taohuayu in Zhengzhou to Hekou Town
　　in Inner Mongolia　　　　　　　　　　　　　　　　　　　　　013
　　Ⅲ. The Downstream: Tracing to the Sea　　　　　　　　　　　025

第二章　萌芽与成长：九曲黄河万里沙　　　　　　037
　　一、黄河文化的曙光：新石器时代早期文明的萌芽　　038
　　二、大河岸边大河村：新石器时代黄河文化的发展　　046
　　三、黄河大改道、大禹治水与国家的诞生　　　　　　058

Chapter 2　Germination and Growth: Thousands of Bends, Miles of Sand　　037
　　Ⅰ. The Dawn of the Yellow River Culture: the Buds of the Early
　　Neolithic Civilization　　　　　　　　　　　　　　　　　　　039
　　Ⅱ. Dahe Village on the Bank of the Yellow River: Development
　　of the Yellow River Culture in the Neolithic Age　　　　　　047
　　Ⅲ. The Great Diversion of the Yellow River, Dayu's Water Control
　　and the Birth of the Country　　　　　　　　　　　　　　　059

第三章　根与魂：黄河当中流　067
　　一、寻根往河洛：老家河南的向往　068
　　二、铸魂在中原：文明成就的核心　078
　　三、分久必合：多民族统一国家的壮大与发展　122

Chapter 3　Root and Soul: the Yellow River Flowing in the Middle　067
　　Ⅰ. Finding Roots in Heluo Basin: the Yearning of Our Hometown in Henan　069
　　Ⅱ. Soul-casting in the Central Plains: Core of Civilization Achievements　079
　　Ⅲ. Unifications and Divisions: the Growth and Development of a Multi-ethnic Unified Country　123

第四章　熔铸与再生：奔流到海不复回　137
　　一、开枝散叶：黄河文化的北移南徙　138
　　二、兼容并蓄：异质文化之借鉴吸收　154
　　三、光芒四射：黄河文化的域外影响　168
　　四、生生不息：黄河文化的再生与创新精神　180

Chapter 4　Fusion and Revival: an Irreversible Trend　137
　　Ⅰ. The Northward and Southward Spread of the Yellow River Culture　139
　　Ⅱ. Inclusiveness and Incorporation: Absorption of Heterogeneous Culture　155
　　Ⅲ. Brilliance and Glory: Influence of the Yellow River Culture on Foreign Countries　169
　　Ⅳ. Everlasting Growth: Spirit of Regeneration and Creativity of the Yellow River Culture　181

附录：中国历史年代简表　190
Appendix: A Brief Chronology of Chinese History　190

第一章

孕育：黄河远上白云间

Chapter 1

Breed: the Yellow River Coming Far from the

White Clouds

在人类文明发展的历史长河中，古巴比伦、古埃及、古印度和古中国以其文明起源早、规模大、发展迅速的特点，并称世界四大文明古国。这四大古文明都诞生于大河沿岸，分别是两河流域、尼罗河流域、恒河流域、黄河流域，均为典型的大河农业文明，作为世界文明早期的原生文明，出现了最早的农业、手工业、城市、文字和王权制国家，对临近地区文明的发展产生了重要的影响。

世界早期古文明大都诞生于大河流域的中下游地区，与其适宜人类定居的优越地理环境有密切的关系。受河流定期泛滥的影响，大河流域中下游多为土地肥沃的冲积平原，气候温和，动植物资源丰富，能够满足大量人口定居的需要，故而产生了最早的农业。农业文明的发展迫切需要对河流的大规模治理，需要集中调动周边大量的人力、物力，整合区域政治力量，从而促使了人类早期王权制国家的形成和发展。

其他世界早期的大河文明，多随着外族入侵或异质文明的冲击，逐步消失在历史的长河之中。唯有中国古老的黄河文明，延续至今绵延不绝，形成5000年未断裂的伟大文明史。历史记载和当代考古发现的双重证据表明，中华文明形成在距今约5000年的黄河流域中游地区。在此区域内，有黄河泥沙淤积形成的大面积沃野平原，丘陵台地、森林山地错杂分布，水源充足，温暖湿润，十分适合农业定居文明的形成和发展。黄河中游地区文明作为核心，和黄河上游、下游地区的古代文明一起，宛若群星闪耀，逐步形成了具备多样化特征又有统一本质特色的黄河文明，以悠久光辉的形象屹立于世界文明之林。

黄河发源于巍然高耸、白雪皑皑的巴颜喀拉山，九曲十八弯，蜿蜒5460余千米，流经青海、四川、甘肃、宁夏、内蒙古、陕西、山西、河南、山东九省，流域面积75万多平方千米，在山东利津注入渤海。黄河流经中国青藏高原、黄土高原、华北平原三大地形阶梯，奔腾澎湃、浩荡激昂，成为中华民族百折不挠、坚韧不屈的民族精神代表。下面我们从黄河源头开始，顺流娓娓而行，开启上、中、下游的三段黄河之旅！

In the long history of human civilization, the ancient civilizations of Ancient Babylon, Ancient Egypt, Ancient India, and Ancient China are known as the four ancient civilizations in the world because of their early origins, large scale and rapid development. Born along the banks of large rivers of the Mesopotamia, the Nile River, the Ganges River, and the Yellow River respectively, these four ancient civilizations are all typical large river agricultural civilizations. As primitive civilizations, they gave birth to the earliest agriculture, handicrafts industry, cities, words or characters, and kingdom, producing an important impact on the development of civilizations in neighboring areas.

Most of the early ancient civilizations of the world were born in the middle and lower reaches of the great river basins, which were closely related to the superior geographical environment suitable for human settlement. Affected by the regular flooding of rivers, these places were mostly alluvial plains with fertile land, mild climate and rich animal and plant resources, which could meet the needs of a large number of people to settle down, hence the earliest agriculture was born. The development of agricultural civilizations urgently needs the large-scale management of rivers, which must mobilize a large number of manpower and material resources in the surrounding areas, and integrate the regional political forces, thus promoting the formation and development of early kingdoms.

The other early large river civilizations of the world gradually disappeared, mostly because of the foreign invasions or the impact of heterogeneous civilizations. Only the ancient Yellow River civilization in China has continued to today, shaping a 5,000-year unbroken history of a great civilization. The dual evidences of historical records and contemporary archaeological discoveries indicate that the Chinese civilization was established in the middle reaches of the Yellow River Basin about 5,000 years ago. There are a large area of fertile plains produced by the sedimentation of the Yellow River, hilly platforms, forests and mountains scatter all around, and there are also sufficient water sources, and warm and humid climate, which are very suitable for the formation and development of agricultural settlement civilization. The civilization of the middle reaches as the core, along with those of the upper and lower reaches, has eventually formed the great Yellow River civilization. The Yellow River civilization, diverse and unified, stands in the forest of world civilizations with a venerable and glorious image.

河源之水 摄影/陈维达
The headwater of the Yellow River (photo by Chen Weida)

一、上游：河源高悬云山外

1. 洁净美丽的高原：湿地、湖泊与草原

从内蒙古托克托县河口镇向西，黄河在经过内蒙古河套平原后再折向南进入宁夏平原，沿黄河西南出宁夏平原后就会进入今甘肃省境内，甘肃兰州以西黄河沿黄土高原西北缘奔流，即将登上世界屋脊——青藏高原。以青海贵德为界，黄河上游又可分为河源区和上游区两大区域，黄河上游区从青海贵德以下至内蒙古河口镇，而贵德以上则为河源区。黄河河源在巴颜喀拉山的各姿各雅山东麓，这里海拔5000余米，各姿各雅在藏语中意为雄伟美丽的山。在各姿各雅山的东麓分布着三条名为各姿各雅贡玛、各姿各雅巴玛和各姿各雅尕玛的山沟，从各条大小不等的山沟里涌出清澈的山泉，淙淙山泉汇成小溪。由于小溪在洪水季节常呈红黄色，藏语称之为卡日曲，意思是红铜色的河。卡日曲沿途吸纳了众多溪流，又与黄河北源的约古宗列曲汇合，卡日曲与约古宗列曲汇合后称为玛曲河，意为孔雀河，是黄河源头最初的河道。玛曲河继续东流约20千米，先后进入扎陵湖和鄂陵湖（图1-1）。扎陵湖面积526平方千米，又称"查灵海"，藏语意为白色长湖。鄂陵湖面积628平方千米，水深达9—30米，海拔3300余米，蓄水量在100亿至120亿立方米，又称"鄂灵海"，古称柏海，藏语称错鄂朗，意为蓝色长湖，西距扎陵湖15千米。鄂陵湖形如金钟，东西窄、南北长，鄂陵湖与扎陵湖由一天然堤相隔，形似蝴蝶。这两个淡水湖均位于青海果洛藏族自治州玛多县境，合称为"黄河源头姊妹湖"。青海玛多县被称为"万里黄河第一县"，海拔在4100米左右，黄河上源玛曲河、扎陵湖、鄂陵湖含沙量极少，每当春天来临，嫩草与新绿并茂，漫步在比白头山天池还高出约1500米的两湖之滨，游鱼与飞鸟相映，蓝天共白云相邀，到处是一片生机盎然的景象。待从扎陵、鄂陵两湖流出，黄河已成为滔滔大水，远远望去，仿佛白云天边，水流滔滔。

The Yellow River originates from the towering, snow-capped Bayan Har Mountain. With many branches and bends, winding more than 5,460 kilometers, it flows through the nine provinces of Qinghai, Sichuan, Gansu, Ningxia, Inner Mongolia, Shaanxi, Shanxi, Henan, and Shandong, covers an area of more than 750,000 square kilometers, and injects into the Bohai Sea in Lijin, Shandong. Flowing through the three major terrain steps of China's Qinghai-Tibet Plateau, the Loess Plateau and the North China Plain in a surging, mighty and passionate manner, it has become the representative of the Chinese nation's perseverance. Let us start from the source of it and walk along the Yellow River to start the journey of the upper, middle and lower reaches of it!

Ⅰ. The Upstream: High above the Mountains and the Clouds Is the Source of the Yellow River

1.Clean and Beautiful Plateau: Wetlands, Lakes and Grasslands

From Hekou Town, Tuoketuo County, Inner Mongolia to the west, the Yellow River turns south and enters the Ningxia Plain after passing through the Hetao Plain of Inner Mongolia. After exiting the Ningxia Plain along the southwest of the Yellow River, it enters the territory of today's Gansu Province. To the west of Lanzhou, Gansu, the Yellow River rushes along the northwest of the Loess Plateau, and is about to reach the roof of the world—the Qinghai-Tibet Plateau. Taking Guide in Qinghai as the boundary, the upper reaches of the Yellow River can be divided into two major areas: the riverhead area and the upper reaches. The upper reaches range from Guide in Qinghai to Hekou Town in Inner Mongolia, and the riverhead area covers the west of Guide. The source of the Yellow River lies on the eastern foothills of Gezigeya Mountain of Bayan Har Mountain, which is more than 5,000 meters above sea level. Gezigeya in Tibetan means majestic and beautiful mountains. There are three ravines named Gezigeya Gongma, Gezigeya Bama, and Gezigeya Gama in the eastern foothills of Gezigeya Mountain. Clear springs flow out from the ravines of various sizes, and gurgling springs merge into a small stream. The stream is called "Kariqu" in Tibetan, or "copper-colored river" for its red and yellow appearance during the flood season. Kariqu absorbs many streams along the way, and merges with Yueguzongliequ at the north source of the Yellow River. After the merging, it is

图 1-1　黄河源头区鄂陵湖

Fig. 1-1　Eling Lake in the source area of the Yellow River

2. 古老神圣的河源崇拜：西王母传说

黄河在中国被尊称为"四渎之首"，而黄河源头在中国古代文化中具有十分神圣的地位。在远古中国，黄河被笼统地认为起源于极高峻宽广的"昆仑"神山，传闻高有 5000 千米，周长 1500 千米。昆仑之上是神仙之所，有巍峨的宫阙和无数奇花异草，生长着不死之树。在远古众多神话中，昆仑西王母的传说尤为著名，后世对西王母的崇拜经久不衰。中国最早的神话集《山海经》中记载，西王母为人形、虎齿、豹尾，蓬发戴面具的半神半人形象，掌管人间灾害和刑罚，充满原始宗教的神

called Maqu River, which means Peacock River, and is the original river course at the source of the Yellow River. The Maqu River continues to flow eastward for about 20 kilometers and enters Zhaling Lake and Eling Lake successively (Fig.1-1). Zhaling Lake covers an area of 526 square kilometers, also called "Zhaling Sea," which means the white long lake in Tibetan. Eling Lake's area is 628 square kilometers, 9 to 30 meters in depth and over 3,300 meters above sea level, and has a water storage capacity of 10 billion to 12 billion cubic meters. It is also called Elinghai, Baihai in ancient times, and Cuo Elang in Tibetan which means the blue long lake, 15 kilometers east of Zhaling Lake. Eling Lake is shaped like a golden bell, narrow from east to west, and long from north to south. Eling Lake and Zhaling Lake are separated by a natural embankment like a butterfly. Located in Maduo County of the Guoluo Tibetan Autonomous Prefecture in Qinghai, these

秘狰狞色彩。在秦汉以后，西王母逐渐演变为主管女性生育、拥有使人长生不老灵药的女神形象，有捣炼仙药的玉兔和九尾神狐与之相伴（图1-2），并逐渐成为后世中国道教中地位显赫无比的女仙之宗。对昆仑西王母的崇拜，显现出中国古代先民对黄河源头代表的生命之源、生命归宿的原始崇拜，以及进一步实现生命永恒的理想想象。

图 1-2　西王母汉画像砖（四川新都出土）
Fig. 1-2　A brick with portrait of the West Queen of the Han Dynasty (excavated in Xindu, Sichuan)

two freshwater lakes are collectively called "Sister Lakes at the Source of the Yellow River." Qinghai Maduo County is known as the first county of the Yellow River of thousands of "li" (the Chinese traditional measurement unit which means half of one kilometer), with an elevation of about 4,100 meters. Maqu River, Zhaling Lake and Eling Lake located in the upper source of the Yellow River contain very little sand. Walking along the shores of the two lakes about 1,500 meters higher than Tianchi of the Baitou Mountain in early spring, you will find a vibrant and refreshing scenery. Fresh green turns to be prosperous, fishes and birds are playing briskly, and scattered pure clouds make the blue sky more beautiful. When flowing out from the Zhaling and Eling lakes, the Yellow River has become torrential waves, just like flowing alongside the clouds in the sky seen from a distance.

2. The Ancient Sacred Worship of the Source of the Yellow River: the Legend of the West Queen

The Yellow River is honored as "the top of the Four Rivers" in China, and the source of the Yellow River is very sacred in ancient Chinese culture. In ancient China, the Yellow River is generally considered to have originated from the extremely tall and wide "Kunlun" Mountain, a holy mountain, which is said to be 5,000 kilometers high and 1,500 kilometers in circumference. Kunlun is the place of immortals, with majestic palaces, countless exotic flowers and plants, and undead trees. Among many myths in ancient times, the legend of the West Queen of Kunlun is particularly famous, and the worship of her is enduring. The earliest collection of Chinese mythology *The Classic of Mountains and Rivers* records that the West Queen is a tiger-toothed, leopard-tailed humanoid with disheveled hair and a mask. She is in charge of human disasters and punishments, full of the mysterious and hideous color of primitive religion. After the Qin and Han dynasties, the West Queen gradually evolved into the image of a goddess in charge of female fertility, possessing the elixir of immortality, accompanied by the nine-tailed fox and the jade rabbit who made the elixir (Fig.1-2), and became the most prominent female fairy of the later Chinese Taoism sect in China. The worship of the West Queen of Kunlun shows ancient Chinese ancestors' primitive worship of the source and the destination of life represented by the source of the Yellow River, as well as the wish for imperishable life.

二、中游：郑州桃花峪到河口镇

1."铜头铁尾豆腐腰"：善淤易徙的黄河中游地质特征

从郑州桃花峪溯黄河而上，到内蒙古托克托县河口镇为黄河的中游河段。这一河段黄河蜿蜒曲折于黄土高原之上，已然攀上了东亚大陆的第二级梯段。在东亚大陆的第二阶梯上，海拔 1000—1500 米的黄土高原成为黄河流经的主体区域，这一段黄河干流流经内蒙古、山西、陕西、河南四省区，总长约为 1206 千米，流域面积 34.4 万平方千米（图 1-3），分别占黄河的 22.1% 和 45.7%。黄土高原成为黄河泥沙的主要来源区，以黄河中游起点内蒙古托克托县河口镇到晋陕峡谷最南端的龙门一段而言，这一段黄河河道长 702 千米，落差 654 米，黄河在这里切穿了黄土高原。不仅如此，黄河谷两侧还有壁立竣险的陡崖，这些陡崖往往高出河道面达 100 米以上，形成了著称于世的晋陕大峡谷（图 1-4）。这一段流域面积虽然只有 13.2 万平方千米，径流仅 73 亿立方米，但输沙量达 8.5 亿吨，占全河总输沙量的 53%。龙门以下，黄河左右两岸又有渭河、泾河、汾河、涑河、伊洛河等支流汇入，这些支流多源出黄土高原，含

图 1-3　黄河中游示意图（吴滨滨绘图）

Fig. 1-3　Schematic diagram of the middle reaches of the Yellow River (drawn by Wu Binbin)

II. The Midstream: from Taohuayu in Zhengzhou to Hekou Town in Inner Mongolia

1."Copper Head, Iron Tail and Tofu Waist" Which Means the Two Ends Are Solid While the Middle Is Soft: the Geological Characteristics of the Middle Reaches of the Yellow River That Are Prone to Silting and Migration

From Taohuayu in Zhengzhou to Hekou Town of Tuoketuo County in Inner Mongolia, is the middle reaches of the Yellow River. This section meanders over the Loess Plateau and climbs the second step of the East Asian Continent. On the second step of the East Asian Continent, the Loess Plateau with an altitude of 1,000-1,500 meters turns into the main area through which the Yellow River flows. This section flows through the four provinces of Inner Mongolia, Shanxi, Shaanxi, and Henan, with a total length of about 1,206 kilometers, and covers an area of 344,000 square kilometers (Fig.1-3), accounting for 22.1% and 45.7% of the Yellow River respectively. The Loess Plateau has become the main source of sediment of the Yellow River. From Hekou Town, the beginning of the middle reaches of the Yellow River, to Longmen at the southern end of the Jin-Shaan Grand Canyon, is 702 kilometers long with a drop height of 654 meters, cutting through the Loess Plateau here. Additionally, there are steep cliffs which are often more than 100 meters above the river surface on both sides of the Yellow River Valley, shaping the world-famous Jin-Shaan Grand Canyon (Fig.1-4). The area of this section is only 132,000 square kilometers and the runoff is only 7.3 billion cubic meters, but the sediment transport volume is 850 million tons, accounting for 53% of the total. Longmen's downstream area, the Wei River, the Jing River, the Fen River, the Su River, the Yiluo River and other tributaries flow into the Yellow River on both sides. These tributaries mostly originate from the Loess Plateau and contain a lot of sand. Therefore, when the Yellow River leaves the Loess Plateau and enters the lower reaches of the Great Plain in Shaanxian County, Sanmenxia City, Henan Province, the sediment concentration in the River reaches an average of 36.9 kilograms per cubic meter, which is 7-8 times higher than that in Hekou Town at the beginning of the middle reaches, with the annual sediment transport volume of about 1.6 billion tons. In short, 90% of the sediment in the Yellow River comes from the Loess Plateau.

沙量很高。因此，当黄河离开黄土高原而入下游大平原河南三门峡陕县时，河水中的含沙浓度平均达每立方米36.9千克，这一含沙浓度较中游起点的河口镇的含沙浓度高出7—8倍，年输沙量达16亿吨左右。总之，黄河中90%的泥沙都是来自黄土高原。

龙门以下经陕西潼关至于郑州桃花峪是黄河中游较为特殊的河段，这段河道既有宽河又有窄谷。龙门以下黄河沿关中平原的东缘南流，黄河在此不仅拥有宽阔的河床，而且主流经常摆动漫流，所谓"三十年河东，三十年河西"就是对这一段黄河河性的概括。唐人王之涣则更以"欲穷千里目，更上一层楼"的绝句描绘黄河此段河道的壮阔与豪迈。

2. 三门峡与大禹劈山之传说

黄河自龙门至潼关，由于受到秦岭山脉的阻挡便在潼关转了个大弯，然后一刻不停地向东进入山西、河南两省之间，晋、豫间黄河谷地狭窄异常，水流湍急，河南境内的三门峡就是一段闻名于世的黄河峡谷（图1-5）。黄河流至三门峡段，侧河两岸的石崖像巨钳一样伸入河道，使河谷异常狭窄。不仅如此，黄河河道中又有两大岩石岛并排立于浊流之中，河水被分成三股，水势更加汹涌，三股浊流所经号称鬼门、神门和人门，三门峡之名即由此而来（图1-6）。鬼门和神门意指此处水流湍急，非鬼、神不能通过。人门的水流虽较鬼门、神门稍稍平缓，但驾船由此而过仍然常有生命危险，历来被人们视为畏途。经由鬼门、神门和人门的三股急流在峡谷口合为一股更为汹涌的激流后，迎面又遇到一座岩石小山，"山见水中若柱然"。滚滚浊流冲向若柱小山，发出撼天动地的巨响，这一"柱然小山"被称为"砥柱石"或"中流砥柱"，屹立在黄河的狂澜之中。黄河三门峡段壮观的自然景色赋予炎黄子孙无穷的想象，古人都认为三门峡是大禹治水时劈石裂谷开凿的，故三门峡又有"禹门口"之称。大禹在治水中百折不挠、勇往直前的精神，千百年来也激励着黄河儿女面对困难顽强拼搏、奋斗不息！

图1-4 龙门最窄处只有三十八米（孟宪明摄影）
Fig.1-4 The narrowest part of Longmen, which is only 38 meters wide (photo by Meng Xianming)

Longmen's downstream area, from Tongguan in Shaanxi to Taohuayu of Zhengzhou in Henan, is a relatively special section of the middle reaches of the Yellow River, because there are both wide rivers and narrow valleys. In Longmen's downstream area, the Yellow River flows southward along the east edge of the Guanzhong Plain. The Yellow River in this part has a wide riverbed, and the main river meanders. The so-called "thirty years in the east, and then thirty years in the west," which indicates a dramatic change, is just a summary of the characteristic of this section. The poet Wang Zhihuan of the Tang Dynasty even described the magnificence and grandeur of the Yellow River with "You can enjoy a grander sight by climbing to a greater height" in his quatrain.

图1-5 三门峡的黄河
Fig.1-5 The Yellow River in the part of Sanmen Gorge

图1-6 吴作人油画《黄河三门峡》
Fig.1-6 Oil painting *Sanmen Gorge in the Yellow River* by Wu Zuoren

2. The Legend of Sanmen Gorge and Dayu's Splitting the Mountain

When flowing from Longmen to Tongguan, blocked by the Qinling Mountains, the Yellow River makes a large turn at Tongguan, and then keeps going eastward to enter the place between Shanxi and Henan provinces (Fig. 1-5). The valleys of the Yellow River between Shanxi and Henan are extremely narrow and the water flows dramatically fast. Sanmen Gorge in the territory of Henan is just a section of the world-famous Yellow River Canyon. When it comes to Sanmen Gorge, the stone cliffs on both sides of the side river extend into the river like giant pincers, making the valley extremely narrow. In addition, there are two large rock islands standing side by side in the turbid current in the Yellow River. So the water is divided into three streams, becoming more turbulent. The three turbid currents are known as ghost gate, god gate and human gate, and that's where the name Sanmen Gorge which means the three-gate gorge in Chinese comes from (Fig. 1-6). The ghost gate and the god gate mean that the water here is so turbulent that only ghosts and gods can pass through. Although the current of the human gate is slightly gentler than those of the ghost gate and god gate, there is still life-threatening danger if one passes by boat, so it has always been regarded as a daunting way. After passing through these three gates, the three rapids merge into a more turbulent torrent at the mouth of the canyon. Then this torrent encounters a rocky hill, and "the hill in the water is just like pillars rising straight up." (Li Daoyuan's *Notes on Book of Waterways*) The billowing turbid current rushes towards the hill, making a loud noise that shakes the sky and the earth. This "pillar-like hill" is called the "mainstay stone" or "mainstay" which means it stands in the turmoil of the Yellow River. The magnificent natural scenery of Sanmen Gorge section of the Yellow River gives Chinese people endless imagination. The ancients believed that Sanmen Gorge was excavated by Dayu (Yu the Great), the first emperor of the Xia Dynasty, who split the stone during his flood control, so Sanmen Gorge is also known as Yumenkou, meaning Dayu's gate. Dayu's courage and perseverance in flood control have inspired the people living along the Yellow River to fight hard in the face of difficulties for thousands of years!

黄河小浪底水库黄鹿岛 摄影/董保华
Huanglu Island at Xiaolangdi Reservoir in the Yellow River (photo by Dong Baohua)

3. 河水之清与君主圣德

黄河中游地区流经山西、陕西交界之黄土高原，黄土易于被流水侵蚀，黄河泥沙含量在此骤增，颜色变得浑浊泛黄，"黄河"之名由此而来。而黄河侧蚀带来的河道崩塌、左右摆动给中游两岸的人居安全、农业生产带来威胁，而大量的泥沙淤积亦对下游地区带来极大危害。中国古代人民很早就认识到黄河浑浊、泥沙淤积的弊端，若河水清澈，则预示着河道平稳，人民可以安居乐业。3000多年前周代人即作诗哀叹："俟河之清，人寿几何！"感慨如果等到黄河水变得清澈，不知要经历多少年的沧桑变迁！随着汉代儒家"天人感应"思想的确立，天文气象、自然环境的异常被统治阶层认为是社会秩序重大改变的上天预示。黄河之水由浑浊变得清澈，代表着统治中国的君主具有贤良的品德，是代表天命之所在，能够在治理国家时施行仁政，是值得大书特书的祥瑞之兆。唐代诗人"河清海晏，时和岁丰"这一观念脍炙人口，得到知识阶层及普通民众的普遍认可（图1-7）。黄河水清与君主圣德紧密关联，历代中国皇帝十分重视黄河之水的清浊变化，并以此衡量现实政治之得失，这成为古代中国一个独特而饶有趣味的政治文化现象。

图 1-7　清乾隆宫廷御用霁蓝粉彩海晏河清瓷尊（故宫博物院藏）

Fig.1-7　Emperor Qianlong's Imperial Blue Famille Rose Haiyan-heqing Porcelain Zun (a wine vessel) of the Qing Dynasty (collection of the Palace Museum)

3. The Clearness of the River and the Holy Virtue of the Emperor

The middle reaches of the Yellow River flow through the Loess Plateau at the junction of Shanxi and Shaanxi. The loess is easily eroded by flowing water, so the sediment content of the Yellow River increases sharply here and the color becomes turbid and yellow, which is where the name "Yellow River" comes from. The collapse and swing caused by the lateral erosion of the Yellow River threaten the safety of human settlements and agricultural production on both sides of the middle reaches, and the large amount of sedimentation also brings great harm to the downstream areas. Ancient Chinese people have realized the disadvantages of the turbidity and sedimentation of the Yellow River long before. Clear water indicates that the Yellow River is stable and the people can live and work in peace. More than 3,000 years ago, the poet of the Zhou Dynasty wrote a poem and lamented "How short the life of human is! How long the wait for the Yellow River becoming clear is!", which means it will experience numerous years of profound changes before the Yellow River becomes clear. Following the Confucian interest in "the interaction between man and nature" during the Han Dynasty, abnormal astronomy, weather, or natural events were regarded by the ruling class as a sign of major changes in social order. If the water of the Yellow River changed from turbid to clear, they believed it meant the monarch as the god's representative had a virtuous character and would exercise benevolent governance when ruling the country, which was an auspicious omen worthy of special mention in the history. The idea that the Yellow River turning clear and calm, or "Heqing-haiyan," portends a world of peace and prosperity can be found in a popular Tang Dynasty poem and was widely accepted by the intellectuals and ordinary people (Fig.1-7). The clear water of the Yellow River was closely related to the monarch's virtue, so the emperors of different dynasties all attached great importance to the clarity change of the Yellow River to measure the gains and losses of political power, which became a unique and interesting political and cultural phenomenon in ancient China.

4. "河出图，洛出书"与河洛文化崇拜

中国儒家经典《易经》有"河出图，洛出书，圣人则之"之说。后世之儒家学者逐渐增饰附会，认为"河图"与"洛书"这两幅古代圣人流传下来的神秘图案，蕴含着天下兴衰的深奥含义（图1-8）。"河图""洛书"如果现世，就预示着圣人的出现和国运的兴隆。

传闻在中国上古时代的河洛盆地（今河南省洛阳市境内），有龙形之马背负"河图"，浮出在孟津县黄河之中，献给上古中国"三皇"之首——伏羲，伏羲据此创制"八卦"，成为儒家典籍《周易》之肇始。又传有神龟浮出于洛宁县洛河中，身背"洛书"，献给正在治理洪水的大禹，大禹借治水成功，区划天下九州，成功开创中国第一个古代王权制国家——夏朝。

"河图"与"洛书"虽然带有明显的迷信传闻色彩，亦成为后世中国占卜学说——阴阳五行术的理论源头，但其亦折射出了黄河中游的河洛盆地在中国早期文明中的核心地位。"河图""洛书"历来被认为是河洛文化的滥觞，河洛文化在后世中国成为华夏文化的正统代表，受到历代中华儿女的崇拜和敬仰。

图 1-8 河图洛书与《周易》八卦对应图

Fig.1-8 Corresponding diagrams between He Tu & Luo Shu and the Eight Diagrams in *The Book of Changes*

4. "The Yellow River Produces the Picture While the Luo River Produces the Book" and the Worship of Heluo Culture

The Chinese Confucian classic work *The Book of Changes* includes a saying that "the Yellow River produces the picture while the Luo River produces the book, and the saint Fuxi creates 'the Eight Diagrams' according to them." Later Confucian scholars gradually added their associations to it, believing that the two mysterious patterns of the picture, also named "He Tu," and the book, also named "Luo Shu," which both had been handed down by ancient saints, contained the profound meaning of the rise and fall of the world (Fig.1-8). If the "He Tu" and "Luo Shu" appeared, that would herald the emergence of the saint and the prosperity of the country.

It is said that in the Heluo Basin of ancient China (in Luoyang City, Henan Province today), a dragon-shaped horse carrying a picture, later known as "He Tu, the picture the Yellow River produces," emerged in the Yellow River in Mengjin County, and dedicated it to Fuxi, head of "the Three Primordial Sovereigns: Fuxi, Shennong, and Huangdi (Fuxi, Suiren, and Shennong)" of ancient China. Fuxi created "the Eight Diagrams" accordingly, which became the origin of the Confucian classic *The Book of Changes*. It is also said that a magical turtle floated in the Luo River in Luoning County, carrying a book, later known as "Luo Shu, the book the Luo River produces," and dedicated it to Dayu who was fighting the flood. After the success of flood control, Dayu divided China into nine parts and successfully created China's first ancient kingdom—the Xia Dynasty.

Although "He Tu" and "Luo Shu" are, to some extent, superstitious and legendany, they are still the theoretical source of the later Chinese divination doctrine—Yin-yang and Five-element Thoughts, and have reflected the core position of the Heluo Basin in the middle reaches of the Yellow River in the early Chinese civilization. "He Tu" and "Luo Shu" have always been regarded as the origin of Heluo Culture, and Heluo Culture has become the orthodox representative of Chinese culture in later generations, being worshiped by Chinese descendants since then.

三、下游:入海口溯源

1. 改道与治理:黄河下游河道地理景观的形成

黄河是横亘在东亚大陆上的万里巨川,它的河源在海拔5000余米的青藏高原上,从大河横空的青海高原出发,黄河一路斩万壑,劈千山,九曲十八回,飞流直下,横贯了东亚大陆。黄河尾闾今天在山东东营利津、垦利一带流入渤海(图1-9),在黄河入海口的两侧,晚近以来由于黄河携沙填海形成了广阔的近现代三角洲,这里地势坦平如砥,宛如长带(图1-10)。黄河入海处的海拔高程一般多在3.5米以下,所以,如果站在低平的黄河入海口向西瞭望黄河源头,5500千米以外的高山之巅上,黄河仿佛在天边的白云间逶迤前行,河源与尾闾5000米的巨大落差,又怎能不给人一种"黄河之水天上来,奔流到海不复回"的壮美!

如果以现在山东垦利渔洼为顶点的现代黄河三角洲为起点,溯1855年河南铜瓦厢决口后夺山东大清河入渤海所形成的现行河道而上,1128

图1-9 黄河入海口标志

Fig.1-9 Signs of the Yellow River estuary

III. The Downstream: Tracing to the Sea

1. Diversion and Governance: the Formation of the Geographic Landscape of the Lower Reaches of the Yellow River

The Yellow River is a giant river, spanning tens of thousands of miles on the East Asian Continent. Its source is on the Qinghai-Tibet Plateau at an altitude of more than 5,000 meters. Starting from Qinghai Plateau which is full of rivers, the Yellow River cuts tens of thousands of gullies and mountains, with many bends, and flies across the East Asian Continent. The end of the Yellow River today flows into the Bohai Sea in Lijin and Kenli in Dongying, Shandong Province (Fig.1-9). On both sides of the Yellow River estuary, a vast and flat modern delta appeared due to sand reclamation recently (Fig.1-10). The elevation of the Yellow River estuary area is generally below 3.5 meters. Therefore, if you stand at the low and flat Yellow River estuary and look west at the source of the Yellow River, you will find that on the top of the mountain 5,500 kilometers away, the Yellow River seems to zigzag forward among the clouds. And the huge 5,000-meter drop height between the source and the tail of the Yellow River certainly shows the magnificence of "coming from the sky, the Yellow River rushes to the sea and never returns!"

If we start from the modern Yellow River Delta, which takes Yuwa Village in Kenli of Shandong Province as the apex, and go via the current river course formed by the Daqing River in Shandong Province entering the Bohai Sea after the breach of Tongwaxiang in Henan Province in 1855, we'll find the Yellow River followed the south of the current river course, and entered the Yellow Sea via the Huai River between 1128 and 1855. But before 1128, the Yellow River took the north side of the current channel and entered the Bohai Sea through Tianjin. During the 3,000 years before 1949, the Yellow River spread in a fan shape on the Huang-huai-hai Plain which is located in the east part of Taihang Mountain in Shandong, and between the mountainous regions in western Henan and central Shandong, sweeping out from north to south. Historically, the frequent flooding and diversions of the lower Yellow River were concentrated in this area. As the boundary of the third step of the East Asian Continent, the vast Huang-huai-hai

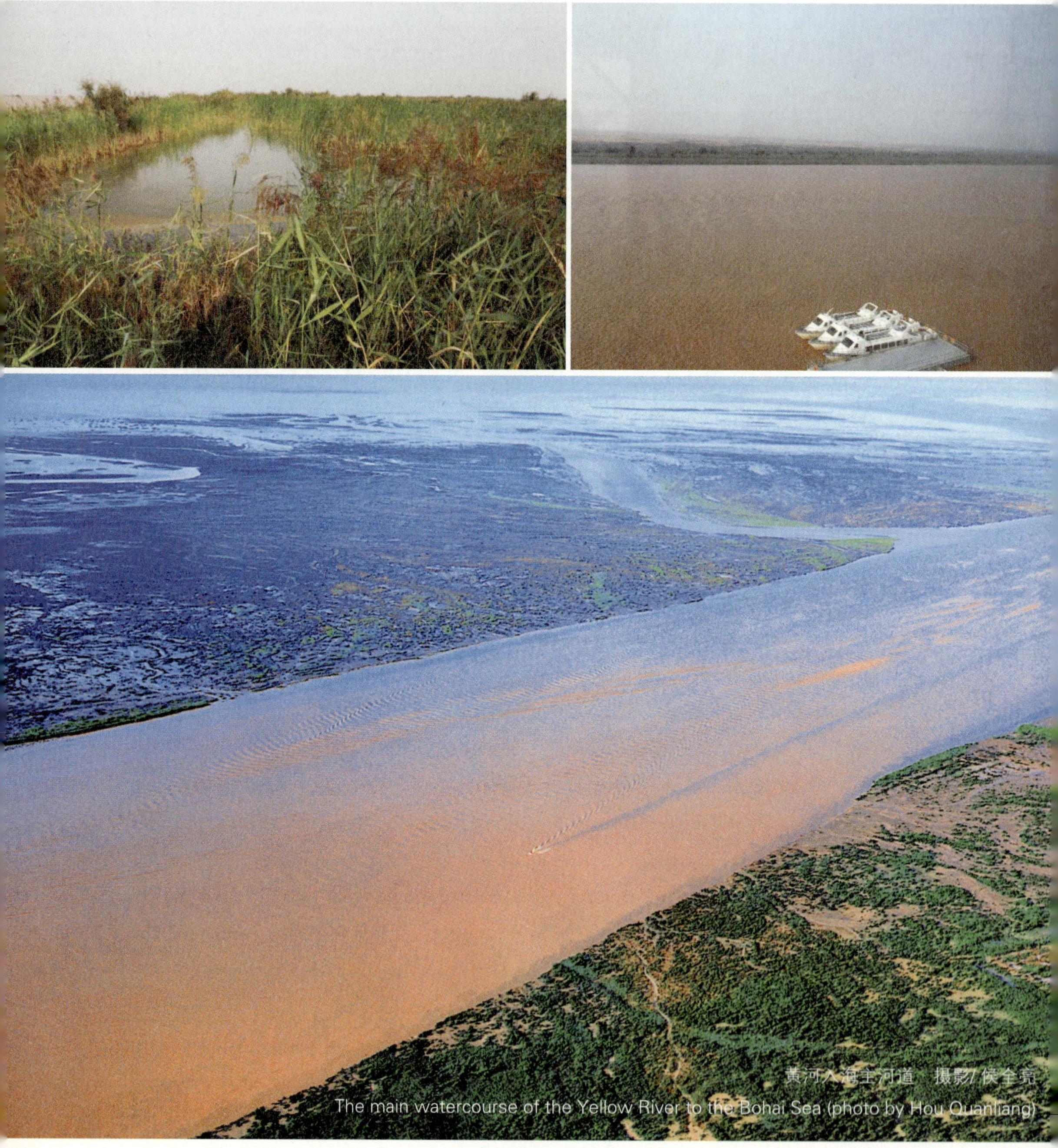

黄河入海主河道 摄影/侯全亮
The main watercourse of the Yellow River to the Bohai Sea (photo by Hou Quanliang)

图 1–10 黄河入海口
Fig.1–10 The Yellow River estuary

Plain is just between the east of Taihang Mountains, Xiao Mountains, Xiong'er Mountains and central Shandong hills and mountainous regions. The coverage from the north to the south of this area is about 250,000 square kilometers, and the altitude is 35-80 meters (Fig. 1-11). This area has suffered from the perfusion of the Yellow River and the silting of the sand from the Yellow River everywhere, and the Yellow River has exerted a huge impact on the geographical environment and the social life of the Huang-huai-hai Plain.

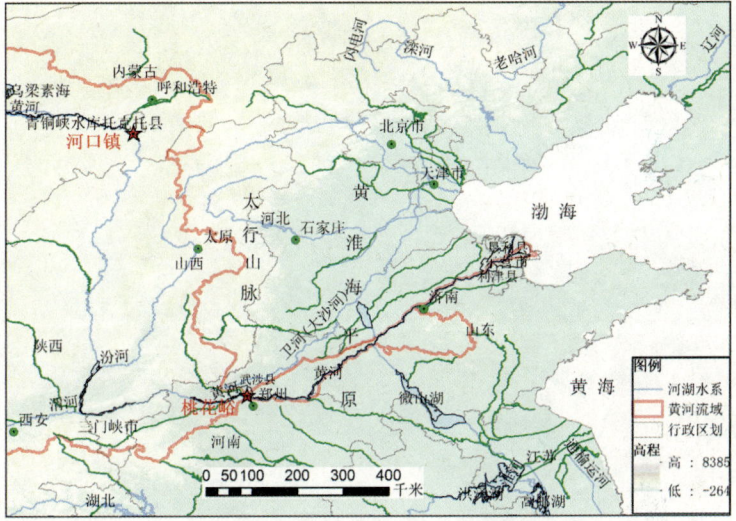

图1-11 黄河下游示意图（吴滨滨绘图）

Fig.1-11 Schematic diagram of the lower reaches of the Yellow River (drawn by Wu Binbin)

Taohuayu on the Mang Mountain in northern Zhengzhou is considered as the starting point of the lower reaches of the Yellow River (Fig.1-12). In Taohuayu's downstream area, the Yellow River has a wide open riverbed, and the broad Yellow River spreads out in an "S" shape on the flat plain. When the flood season comes, the turbid current on the broad river surface is rushing eastward spectacularly. The Yellow River which is to the east of Taohuayu is bound within a long levee of 1,300 kilometers. Now in the south of Wuzhi County, there is an imperial dam with a length of about 1,000 meters connected to the Qin River dam. The imperial dam is on the left (north) bank of the Yellow River, opposite

黄河下游开封黑岗口　摄影 / 董保华
Heigangkou Reservoir in the lower Yellow River, Kaifeng (photo by Dong Baohua)

年至1855年，黄河走现行河道以南经淮河入黄海，而在公元1128年以前，黄河又走现行河道北侧，经过天津入渤海。在1949年以前的3000多年里，黄河在太行山东、豫西山地至山东鲁中山地之间的黄淮海平原上作扇面形状展开，并且自北向南横扫了一遍。历史上，黄河下游频繁的决溢和改道都集中在这个区域，作为东亚大陆第三阶梯的分界处，太行山、崤山、熊耳山以东至鲁中丘陵山地之间就是广阔的黄淮海平原，这一区域的南北纵横大约有25万平方千米，海拔高度在35—80米（图1–11）。这一区域内无处不遭受过黄河水沙的灌注和淤淀，黄河对黄淮海平原的地理环境和社会生活产生过巨大的影响。

郑州北部邙山上的桃花峪被认为是黄河下游河段的起点（图1–12）。桃花峪以下黄河河床开阔，宽阔的黄河大溜呈"S"形展布在平坦的大平原上，洪水季节来临，宽阔的河面上但见滚滚浊流向东奔腾，气势壮观。桃花峪以东的黄河开始被束缚在长达1300千米的长堤之内，现在武陟县南有一段御坝，这段大坝长约1000米，与沁河大坝相连，位于黄河左（北）岸，与右（南）岸郑州邙山上的桃花峪遥遥相对。清朝雍正二年（1724年），黄河大溜受到右（南）岸官庄峪山嘴顶冲，出湾后大溜直注东北方向，顶冲北岸沁、黄交汇处姚期营、秦厂一带，河势险要。为缓解姚期营、秦厂一带险情，便在秦厂一带相度地势，添筑挑水坝，挑溜外行，以保大坝安全。此段大坝是奉雍正皇帝旨修建，坝成后镌立碑石纪念，坝称"御坝"，碑称"御坝碑"，现存于河南武陟县二营铺御坝村（图1–13）。

黄河右左两岸大坝工程之浩大，堪与万里长城、中国大运河相匹比，是中华民族创造的又一伟大奇迹（图1–14，1–15）！

图1-12 桃花峪：黄河中、下游分界线（陈东川摄影）
Fig.1-12 Taohuayu: the boundary between the middle and lower reaches of the Yellow River (photo by Chen Dongchuan)

to Taohuayu on the Mang Mountain in Zhengzhou which is on the right (south) bank. In the second year of the Yongzheng (an emperor of the Qing Dynasty) Period (1724), the Yellow River was overshot by the Guanzhuangyu Mountain on the right (south) bank. After exiting the bay, it went straight to the northeast, and rushed to the area around Yaoqiying and Qinchang at the intersection of the Qin River and the Yellow River on the north bank, and the river regime was dangerous. In order to alleviate the danger in Yaoqiying and Qinchang area, spur dikes were built and the water was led out according to the observance of Qinchang area to keep the dam safe. The dam was built according to the decree of Emperor Yongzheng. After it was completed, a memorial stone was erected. The dam was called "Imperial Dam" and the stele was called "Imperial Dam Stele," which are now in Royal Dam Village of Eryingpu, Wuzhi County, Henan Province (Fig.1- 13).

The huge dam projects on both banks of the Yellow River are comparable to the Great Wall and the Grand Canal of China. It is another great miracle created by the Chinese nation (Fig.1-14, 1-15)!

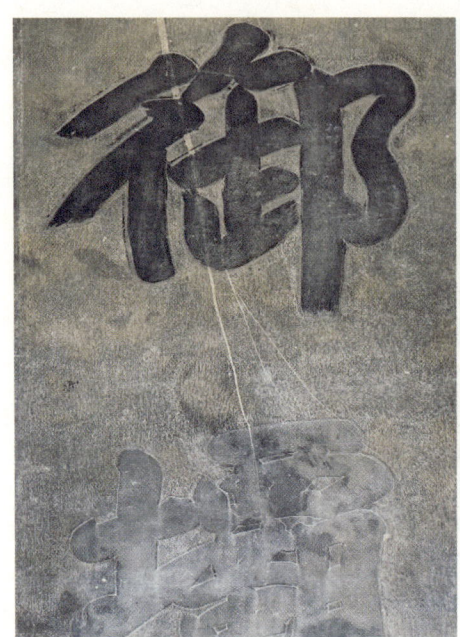

图1-13 雍正黄河御坝碑（陈东川摄影）

Fig.1-13 The Imperial Dam Stele of the Yellow River (photo by Chen Dongchuan)

2. 敬畏与祈福：黄河河神的祭祀传统

历史上黄河的改道多集中在下游的平原地带，每次决口泛滥，淹没无数农田民居，生灵涂炭，给民众带来了深重的苦难。故此，古代黄河下游各阶层人士对黄河有深深的畏惧意识，由畏惧转为敬拜祈福，河神信仰根深蒂固，民间修建的祭祀庙宇众多，香火不绝，并逐步上升到国家层面的官方祭祀。

商代甲骨文中即记载有不少商王定时、定点祭祀黄河的事迹，至周代礼制规定只有周天子才有资格祭祀黄河，黄河河神按照诸侯王级别祭祀。西汉时期黄河祭祀正式列入国家祀典，设立专门的河祠、祠官，公元前132年汉武帝甚至亲至黄河瓠子决口处向黄河水神敬献玉璧、白马，祈求黄河安澜。此后历代直至明清时期，官方对黄河的祭祀传统一直延续下来。

图 1-14 黄河右岸千里长堤起点（陈东川摄影）

Fig.1-14 The starting point of the long dike on the right bank of the Yellow River (photo by Chen Dongchuan)

图 1-15 黄河左岸沁河堤与黄河堤交汇（陈东川摄影）

Fig.1-15 The intersection of the Qin River Dike and the Yellow River Dike on the left bank of the Yellow River (photo by Chen Dongchuan)

2. Awe and Blessing: the Sacrificial Tradition of the Yellow River God

Historically, the diversions of the Yellow River were mostly concentrated in the lower plains. Every time the breach overflowed, it flooded countless farmland

清代康熙、雍正时期，黄河屡次在河南省武陟县决口北流，威胁华北乃至京师之安全。雍正帝特意在武陟县黄河岸边敕建嘉应观，敕封"总领淮黄诸河河神"牌位，为黄河河神按照帝王标准修建行宫祭祀（图1-16）。武陟嘉应观仿制清代故宫格局而建，占地将近900亩，有殿、亭、楼、阁等不同风格建筑300余间，成为黄河流域面积最大、级别最高的河神庙。武陟嘉应观至今犹存，庙宇巍峨壮观，有"黄河小故宫"之美誉。

图 1-16　黄河第一观——河南武陟县嘉应观（陈东川摄影）

Fig.1-16　The First Temple of the Yellow River—the Jiaying Temple in Wuzhi County, Henan Province (photo by Chen Dongchuan)

and houses, and brought the people great sufferings. The people in the lower reaches of the Yellow River in ancient times lived in great fear of the floods, and turned to worship and prayer to river gods for protection. The belief in river gods was so deeply rooted that many worship temples were built with an endless stream of pilgrims, which gradually evolved into official sacrifices at the national level.

The oracle bone inscriptions of the Shang Dynasty recorded many occasions of the kings' offering sacrifices to the Yellow River regularly at fixed time and place. In the Zhou Dynasty, the ritual system stipulated that only the emperor was qualified to worship the Yellow River, and the Yellow River gods were offered sacrifice according to the rank of the feudal lords. In the Western Han Dynasty, the Yellow River sacrifice ceremonies were formally listed into the national ceremonies, and river temples were specially established and officials were specially appointed. In 132 BC of the Western Han Dynasty when the Yellow River burst in Huzi, Emperor Wudi even got there in person, offering jade and white horses to the water god of the Yellow River to pray for the peace. From then on, the official tradition of sacrificing to the Yellow River continued through the Ming and Qing dynasties.

During the Emperor Kangxi and Yongzheng periods of the Qing Dynasty, the Yellow River repeatedly burst and flowed northward in Wuzhi County, Henan Province, threatening the safety of North China and even the capital. Emperor Yongzheng specially built the Jiaying Temple on the bank of the Yellow River in Wuzhi County, awarded the memorial tablet of "the General of the Huai River, the Yellow River, and Other Rivers' Gods," and constructed a palace for the Yellow River god in accordance with the emperor's standards (Fig.1-14). The Jiaying Temple in Wuzhi was built according to the pattern of the Forbidden City in the Qing Dynasty, covering an area of nearly 900 mu, equal to 148 acres. It has more than 300 buildings of different styles, such as halls, towers and pavilions, making it the largest and highest level of river temples in the Yellow River Basin. The Jiaying Temple in Wuzhi County, majestic and magnificent, still exists today, and gets the reputation of "The Little Forbidden City of the Yellow River."

第二章

萌芽与成长：九曲黄河万里沙

Chapter 2

Germination and Growth: Thousands of Bends,

Miles of Sand

一、黄河文化的曙光：新石器时代早期文明的萌芽

黄河文化如同黄河万里绵长。

黄河文化的曙光最先投射在哪里？没有考古资料的证明就很难说清这个问题。但是 2010 年，河南郑州的考古工作者在郑州市新密岳村镇李家沟西发现了距今 10500 年至 8600 年、连续的史前文化堆积。其丰富的文化内涵使我们看到了黄河文化的第一缕曙光。

人类的历史虽然漫长，但是人类社会开始发生重大的改变是在考古学上所说的新石器时代。这一时代有四大特征：农业的出现、动物的驯养、陶器的制作、磨制石器的使用，这四个特征并不一定是同时出现，它们的意义也不尽相同。农业的出现是人类历史上掌握火的使用方法以后的第一次"经济革命"，它使人类由食物采集转变为食物生产，人类社会由此达到了一个新高度；而对动物的驯养则被视为人类农业生产的延续，它进一步丰富完善了人类食物的生产类型；磨制石器的使用则将旧石器时代蕴含的潜能进一步释放出来，给生产力的发展插上了有力的翅膀；陶器的制作使得人类得以更有效地摄取营养，也极大地改变了人类社会，成为判断进入新石器时代最显著的标志物之一。考古发现遗址中出土的上述遗物，可以成为我们判断人类社会物质文化发展水平的标准，同时也可以帮助我们认识黄河流域文化发展的脉络。

只有在黄河流域的古代遗址出现了上述诸多遗物或遗迹，我们才能说真正看到了黄河文化的曙光。

1. 万年曙光：新密李家沟遗址农业定居文明的出现

李家沟遗址，位于河南省新密市岳村镇李家沟西，属于淮河水系溱水河上游的椿板河。虽然自西北向东南流经李家沟遗址的西侧，但李家沟遗址位于嵩山东麓，北距黄河仅 44 千米左右，地势由东北向西南倾斜，

Ⅰ. The Dawn of the Yellow River Culture: the Buds of the Early Neolithic Civilization

The history of the Yellow River culture is as long as the Yellow River itself.

Where did the dawn of the Yellow River culture project first? It is difficult to clarify this problem without evidence of archaeological data. But in 2010, archaeologists in Zhengzhou, Henan Province discovered a continuous accumulation of prehistoric cultures about 10,500 to 8,600 years ago in the west of Lijiagou, Yuecun Town, Xinmi City. Its rich cultural connotation enables us to see the first light of the Yellow River culture.

Although the history of mankind is long, the era when human society began to undergo major changes was the Neolithic Age. This era had four major characteristics: the emergence of agriculture, the domestication of animals, the production of pottery, and the use of polished stone tools. The four characteristics did not necessarily appear at the same time and they also conveyed different meanings. The emergence of agriculture was the first "economic revolution" in human history after they mastered the use method of fire, contributing to the transformation from the food collection period to food production period, hence a new height of human society; the domestication of animals was regarded as the continuation of human agricultural production, which further enriched and improved the types of human food production; grinding stone tools further released the potential contained in the Paleolithic Age and gave powerful wings to the development of productivity; the production of pottery rendered the intake of nutrients more effectively and it also greatly changed human society and became one of the most significant markers for judging the entry of the Neolithic Age. The above-mentioned relics unearthed from the archaeological discovery sites can serve as a standard for us to judge the level of material and cultural development of human society, and can also help us understand the context of cultural development in the Yellow River Basin.

Only when many of the above-mentioned relics appear in ancient sites in the Yellow River Basin can we say that we have truly seen the dawn of the Yellow River culture.

属黄土堆积发育,向东即是黄淮海大平原,我们把这一地区作为研究黄河文化的核心地区应没有问题。

在李家沟遗址中有一处颇具特色的石块聚集区,遗址中心由磨盘、石砧和扁平石块构成,其中还夹杂着大量的烧石碎块、陶片、动物骨骼。动物骨骼中带有明显人工切割过的长骨断口,这些动物骨骼多是食草动物。这一区域中还存在着大量烧石,说明这里应该是一处人类活动相对稳定的居住区域。

在李家沟遗址中发现了200多片陶片,这些陶片均为夹砂粗陶,颜色有浅灰黄色、红褐色,部分陶片质地坚硬,火候较高(图2-1)。这批陶片虽然保留有直口筒形类的陶器特点,但与最原始的制陶技术与风格相比较,李家沟的这批陶片显然不是最原始的器物。

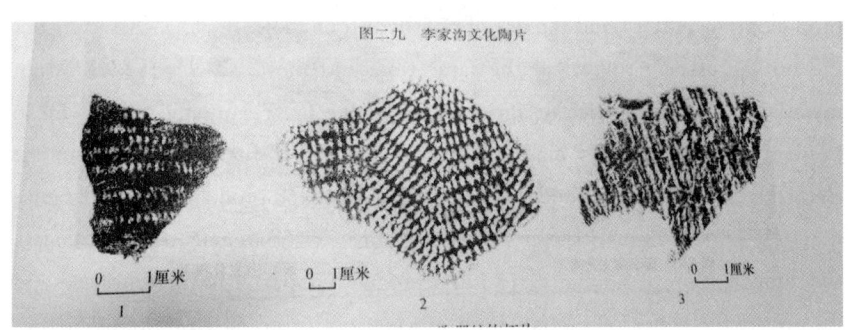

图 2-1 李家沟文化陶器纹饰

王幼平等:《李家沟遗址与旧新石器时代过渡》,科学出版社,2018

Fig. 2-1 Lijiagou Cultural Pottery Decoration

Wang Youping's *Lijiagou Site and the Transition from the Paleolithic Age to the Neolithic Age*, Science Press, 2018

李家沟遗址中发现的石器有石磨盘、石锛、尖状器、刮削器、砍砸器等。从这些石器的组合特征来看,它们显然是用于农业生产的。其中石锛和砍砸器可用于砍伐树木和荆棘,石锛的刃口有砍伐草木使用后留下的明显痕迹。尖状器应该是用来戳地成穴、锥洞点种,这种石器后来发展成为专门的点种播种农具。李家沟遗址中还出土有一件长34厘米、

1. The Dawn Ten Thousand Years Ago: the Emergence of Agricultural Settlement Civilization at the Lijiagou Site in Xinmi

The Lijiagou Site, located in the west of Lijiagou, Yuecun Town, Xinmi City, Henan Province, belongs to the Chunban River which is in the upper reaches of the Qinshui River in the Huai River system. Although the Chunban River flows through the west side of the Lijiagou Site from northwest to southeast, the Lijiagou Site is located on the eastern foothill of the Songshan Mountain, and the north of it is only 44 kilometers far from the Yellow River. Lijiagou Site slopes from the northeast to the southwest and belongs to the accumulation of loess, and to the east of it is the Huang-huai-hai Great Plain. Therefore, it is reasonable for us to regard this area as the core area for studying the Yellow River culture.

There is a distinctive stone gathering area in the Lijiagou Site, of which the center is composed of millstones, stone anvils and flat stones, which are also mixed with a large number of burnt stone fragments, pottery pieces and animal bones. There are obvious long bone fractures cut by human beings in the animal bones, most of which come from herbivores. There are still many burnt rocks in this area, indicating that it should be a relatively stable residential area for human activities.

More than 200 pottery pieces were found in the Lijiagou Site. These pottery pieces, made of sand-filled coarse pottery, have different colors, such as grayish yellow and reddish brown. Some of them are hard in texture, which means they were fired in a high temperature (Fig. 2-1). Although this batch of pottery pieces retains the characteristics of straight-mouthed cylindrical pottery, compared with the techniques and styles of the most primitive pottery, it is obvious that this batch of Lijiagou pottery pieces is not the most primitive.

The stone tools found in the Lijiagou Site include millstones, stone adzes, pointed objects, scrapers, and choppers. Judging from the combined characteristics of these stone tools, they are obviously used for agricultural production. Among them, the stone adze and the chopper can be used to cut down trees and thorns, and the blade of the stone adze has obvious marks left by cutting the grass and wood. The pointed tool should be used to poke a hole into the ground and tap the hole for seeding. This stone tool later developed into a special seeding and planting tool. A millstone measuring 34 centimeters in length and 16.1 centimeters in width was also unearthed from the Lijiagou Site. The surface of the

宽 16.1 厘米的石磨盘，石磨盘表面有加工谷物与其他植物籽粒后留下的痕迹。

目前，我们虽然还无法确切地了解当时的农作物构成状况，但李家沟遗址中这些石器工具组合，使我们有理由推测在距今 10000 年前后的新石器时代早期，黄河与淮河之间的嵩山东麓一带已经存在原始农业了，这一地区已经具备发展农业生产的基本条件。

2. 多姿多彩：裴李岗文化的耕作技术和艺术创造

裴李岗文化，因最先发现于郑州裴李岗而著称于世。裴李岗文化距今 9000—7000 年，较新密李家沟文化晚了 1000—2000 年，但新郑新密两地毗邻，两个文化遗址相距约 18.4 千米（图 2-2）。裴李岗文化的发现使中原地区新石器时代早期考古研究取得了突破性进展。在裴李岗文化的新郑沙窝李遗址中发现过 1—1.5 平方米的粟米碳化颗粒，在许昌丁庄遗址内又发现了脱粒粟米，其干粒重 1.88 克。在贾湖遗址中还发现了许多碳化稻米和稻壳，经过对这些稻米和稻壳形态与硅酸体的分析，考古工作者认为这些稻米和稻壳是以粳稻特征为主、具有原始形态的栽培稻。

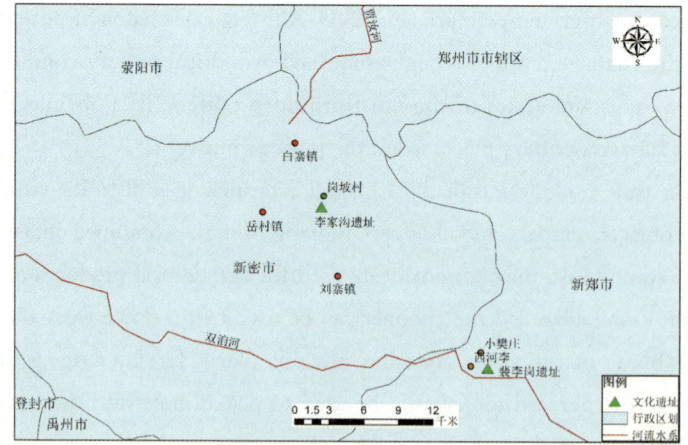

图 2-2　李家沟遗址与裴李岗遗址位置图（吴滨滨绘图）
Fig. 2-2　The Lijiagou Site and the Peiligang Site (drawn by Wu Binbin)

millstone has traces left after processing grains and other plant seeds.

Although we still don't know exactly the kinds of crops at that time, these stone tools at the Lijiagou Site give us reasons to speculate that in the early Neolithic Period around 10,000 years ago, primitive agriculture had already existed in the eastern piedmont of Songshan Mountain which was located between the Yellow River and the Huai River, and this area already had the basic conditions for the development of agricultural production.

2. The Colorful Farming Technology and Artistic Creation of the Peiligang Culture

The Peiligang Culture was shaped 9,000-7,000 years ago, about 1,000-2,000 years later than the Lijiagou Culture of Xinmi. However, Xinzheng and Xinmi are adjacent, and the two cultural sites are about 18.4 kilometers apart (Fig. 2-2). A breakthrough was made in the archaeological research of the early Neolithic Period in the Central China since the discovery of the Peiligang Culture. Carbonized millet spreading in 1-1.5 square meters was found in the Xinzheng Shawoli Site of the Peiligang Culture, and threshing millet was found in the Xuchang Dingzhuang Site, with a dry weight of 1.88 grams. Many carbonized rice and rice husks were also found in the Jiahu Site. After analyzing the form and silicate of these rice and rice husks, archaeologists believe that these rice and rice husks are primitive cultivated rice with the characteristics of japonica rice.

The discovery of millet and rice remains proved that the primitive agriculture in the Yellow River Basin had initially prospered during the Peiligang Culture Period about 8,000 years ago.

Compared with the Lijiagou Culture in Xinmi around 10,000 years ago, the cultural connotation of the Peiligang Culture about 8,000 years ago seems richer and more colorful.

The earliest rice wine and honey in the world were discovered in the pottery unearthed from the Wuyang Jiahu Site of the Peiligang Culture. And more than 30 bone flutes were unearthed from the Jiahu Site, among which a five-hole bone flute has a particularly accurate scale. The high tones emitted by each sound hole of this bone flute completely correspond to the 5/6/1/2/3 of the Pythagorean Tuning System.

粟稻遗存的发现证明，在距今8000年左右的裴李岗文化时期，黄河流域的原始农业已有初步的繁荣。

与距今10000年左右的新密李家沟文化相比，距今8000年左右的裴李岗文化所展现出来的丰富多彩的黄河流域文化内涵，似乎更胜一筹。

在裴李岗文化舞阳贾湖遗址出土的陶器内，发现了世界最早的米酒和蜂蜜。贾湖遗址中出土了三十多支骨笛，其中一只五孔骨笛音阶尤为准确，这只骨笛每个音孔发出的高音与五度相生律制的 5/6/1/2/3 五音完全相同。

贾湖 M282 号墓出土的两支七孔骨笛可以发出七声音阶。在此之前，音乐学者普遍认为七声音阶源自西方，贾湖遗址中七孔骨笛的发现，证明七八千年前，黄河与淮河之间的中国先民确已掌握了七声音阶。现代音乐家甚至可以用它吹出北方民歌《小白菜》，裴李岗文化的进步让后世惊叹！

从两百多万年前开始，到一万年前左右结束的旧石器时代即将画上句号。一万年前，对于人类文化来说可能才是一个真正意义上的起点。黄河岸边这缕已经燃起的曦光，在未来的岁月将会在东亚大陆的原野上投射出灿烂的光辉。

The two seven-hole bone flutes unearthed from Tomb M282 in Jiahu can emit seven-tone scales. Before this, music scholars generally believed that the seven-tone scales originated from the West. The discovery of the seven-hole bone flutes at the Jiahu Site proved that the Chinese ancestors between the Yellow River and the Huai River had indeed mastered the seven-tone scales seven to eight thousand years ago. Modern musicians can even use it to play the Northern folk song *Small Cabbage*. The later generations are amazed by the progress of the Peiligang Culture.

The Paleolithic Age, which began more than 2 million years ago and ended about 10,000 years ago, is about to come to an end. Ten thousand years ago, it may have been a real starting point for human culture. This ray of light on the bank of the Yellow River will shine brightly on the wilderness of East Asia in the years to come.

黄河口湿地丹顶鹤　摄影/董保华
Red-crowned cranes in the Yellow River estuary wetland (photo by Dong Baohua)

二、大河岸边大河村：新石器时代黄河文化的发展

大河村，位于黄河南岸郑州市东北郊柳林镇。从大河村向西南约一千米有一道慢坡土岗，这条土岗呈西南－东北走向，南、北两面坡度较大。旧时岗上盛产棉花，当地群众称之为"花岗"。20 世纪 70 年代，就在这条土岗上发现了著名的大河村遗址，该遗址是黄河流域数千处古遗址中的佼佼者。

大河村遗址的发掘前后经历了 15 年（图 2-3）。考古工作者收集了大河村遗址中 28 个 C-14 年代数据标本后确认大河村仰韶文化上限估计距今 6800 年，下限估计距今 4400—4100 年。按照 C-14 年代数据标本所揭示的年代序列，先民们在黄河岸边延续居住了 3300 年之久。大河村遗址面积 40 多万平方米，文化层堆积厚达 12.5 米。文化内涵异常

图 2-3　大河村遗址（大河村博物馆戴建增馆长供图）
Fig. 2-3　The Dahe Village Site provided by Dai Jianzeng, director of Dahe Village Ruins Museum

II. Dahe Village on the Bank of the Yellow River: Development of the Yellow River Culture in the Neolithic Age

Dahe Village is located in Liulin Town which is in the northeastern suburb of Zhengzhou City on the south bank of the Yellow River. There is a sloping mound 1 kilometer southwest of Dahe Village. This mound is oriented from southwest to northeast, with steep slopes on both sides of the south and north. In the old days, the mound was rich in cotton, therefore the local people called it "Cotton Mound" ("Hua Gang" in Chinese phonetic alphabet). In the 1970s, the famous Dahe Village Site was discovered on this mound, being the most impressive one among thousands of sites in the Yellow River Basin.

The excavation of the Dahe Village Site took 15 years. Archaeologists collected 28 data specimens in C-14 era from the Dahe Village Site and confirmed that the upper limit of the Yangshao Culture in Dahe Village is estimated to be about 6,800 years ago, and the lower limit is estimated to be 4,400-4,100 years ago. According to the chronological sequence revealed by data specimens from the C-14 era, the ancestors had lived on the banks of the Yellow River for 3,300 years (Fig. 2-3). The Dahe Village Site covers an area of more than 400,000 square meters, and its cultural deposit is as thick as 12.5 meters. The cultural connotation, extremely rich, includes not only the Yangshao Culture, the Longshan Culture, the Erlitou Culture and the Shang Culture, but also relics unearthed in the Shandong Dawenkou Culture and the Hubei Qujialing Culture, providing vivid objects for the study of the five thousand years of civilization of the Chinese nation.

1. The Culture of Beautifully Painted Pottery at the Dahe Village Site in Zhengzhou

Painted pottery is the most colorful relic of the Dahe Village Site. The painted pottery of Dahe Village obviously has a process of emergence, development, prosperity and decline. The early colored pottery of the Yangshao Culture of Dahe Village was not only small in number but also simple in patterns with only band-shaped lines and wide banded lines which were colored in single

丰富，不仅包含有仰韶文化、龙山文化、二里头文化和商文化，还出土有山东大汶口文化和湖北屈家岭文化遗物，为研究中华民族五千年文明史提供了生动的实物资料。

1. 郑州大河村遗址绝美彩陶文化

彩陶是大河村遗址最为丰富多彩的遗物。大河村的彩陶显然有一个产生、发展、鼎盛和衰落的过程。大河村仰韶文化的前期彩陶数量少、花纹简单，只有带状和宽带纹，仅有黑、棕、红单彩。经过一段时间的发展，彩陶数量和花纹图案开始增多，花纹图案除施黑、棕、红单彩之外，还有黑红或棕红两彩兼施。再经过千余年的发展，大河村的彩陶文化几乎达到了鼎盛。这一时期，大河村彩陶数量众多，花纹图案繁富，色彩艳丽。花纹图案除沿用以前的固有图案外，还出现了太阳纹、花蕾纹、树叶纹、树形纹、锯齿纹、六角星纹、舟形纹、莲蓬纹、菱形纹、禾苗纹、蝶须纹、木骨纹、豆荚纹、日晕纹等。花纹图案多为黑色、红色或棕、红两彩兼施，单色彩较少。施彩的器形主要有钵、瓮、碗、豆、盆、瓶、罐、壶和陶环等，而且白衣彩陶更为丰富。到了大河村仰韶文化第四期的时候，彩陶开始衰退，白衣彩陶消失，更少见两彩兼施，花纹图案简单草率，直至消失。

穿越漫长的时光隧道，大河村发现的这些彩陶向我们诉说着6000年前黄河岸边大河村先民的生活和他们丰富多彩的内心世界。1972年，在大河村遗址仰韶文化房基下，出土了彩陶双连壶（图2-4）。该壶红衣黑彩，器表布满平行线条图案。两壶并连，腹部相接处有一圆孔相通。壶两侧各附一耳，圆腹平底。它利用连通器原理将两个一样的壶体巧妙地连接在一起，造型别致，构思新颖，器表磨光，涂红衣，饰黑彩平行线13—15周不等，两平行直线纹间又饰三条垂线或斜线纹，线条古朴流畅，风格独特，对研究原始社会的社会形态、生活习俗和制陶艺术有重要价值。

black, brown and red. After a period of development, the number and patterns of the colored pottery began to increase. In addition to the single color of black, brown and red, there were also black-red or brown-red colors. After more than a thousand years of development, the Painted Pottery Culture of Dahe Village almost reached its peak. During this period, Dahe Village boasted a large amount of painted pottery, with rich patterns and various colors. In addition to the previous inherent patterns, there were also sun patterns, flower bud patterns, leaf patterns, tree patterns, zigzag patterns, hexagonal star patterns, boat patterns, lotus patterns, diamond patterns, seedling patterns, butterfly patterns, and wood bones patterns, pod patterns, and solar halo patterns. Patterns were mostly painted in black and red or colored with red and brown. Few of them were in single color. The utensils of the colored pottery mainly included earthen bowls, earthen jars, bowls, compotes, salvers, bottles, jugs, pots and pottery rings, etc. Besides, the white- clothed painted pottery was more abundant. By the time of the fourth phase of the Yangshao Culture in Dahe Village, painted pottery began to decline and white-clothed painted pottery disappeared. The painted pottery with two colors was seldom seen and the patterns were simple and rough.

Through the long time tunnel, the painted pottery found in Dahe Village tells us the life of the ancestors of Dahe Village on the bank of the Yellow River 6,000 years ago and their colorful inner world. In 1972, under the foundation of the Yangshao Culture building at the Dahe Village Site, a painted pottery twin pot was unearthed (Fig. 2-4). The bottom color of the pot was painted in red, but its surface was covered with parallel and black banded lines. The two pots were connected side by side with a circular hole at the junction of the abdomen. There was one ear-shaped handle on each side of the pot with round belly and flat bottom. It used the principle of the communicating vessels to skillfully connect two identical pots together. It had a unique shape and was an ingenious design. The surface of the vessel was polished, painted in red, and decorated with 13-15 black and parallel lines. Three vertical lines or oblique lines were decorated between each pair of parallel straight lines. The lines, simple and smooth, with unique style, are of great value to the study of the social form, living habits and pottery art of primitive society.

According to ethnological data, the twin pot is a ceremonial artifact. The

图 2-4 彩陶双连壶
Fig. 2-4 Painted pottery twin pot

据民族学资料考证,双连壶是一件礼仪用品。大河村和周围其他部落的先民们,在共同的生产活动中互相帮助,相濡以沫,逐渐建立了情同手足的友谊,而双连壶就是氏族结盟或举行重大庆祝活动时氏族首领或长者对饮的酒具,是和平友好的象征。如今,它已成为我国对外交流的使者,带着一个古老民族的心愿,传遍了世界各地。

大河村仰韶文化的彩陶中还有众多月亮纹、太阳纹、日晕纹和彗星纹的天文花纹图案(图2-5)。就月亮纹而言,其组成是相同的,中间饰圆点,圆点纹左右两侧各饰月牙纹。中间圆点纹表示满月,左右两侧

a. 太阳纹(1)　　b. 太阳纹(2)　　c. 月亮纹　　d. 日晕纹
a. sun pattern (1)　b. sun pattern (2)　c. moon pattern　d. solar halo pattern

图 2-5 仰韶文化太阳纹、月亮纹、日晕纹复原图(《郑州大河村》)
Fig. 2-5 Restoration plan of the sun pattern, moon pattern and solar halo pattern of the Yangshao Culture (*Zhengzhou Dahe Village*)

ancestors of Dahe Village and other surrounding tribes helped each other in the common production activities, and gradually established a close friendship. The twin pot was the drinking set used by clan leaders or elders when clan alliances or major celebrations were held. Therefore, it was a symbol of peace and friendship. Today, it has become a messenger of our country's foreign exchanges, spreading all over the world with the wish of an ancient nation.

The painted pottery of the Yangshao Culture of Dahe Village also has many astronomical patterns, such as moon patterns, sun patterns, solar halo patterns and comet patterns (Fig. 2-5). As far as the moon pattern is concerned, the composition is the same, with dots in the middle, and crescent patterns on the left and right sides of the dot pattern. The dot pattern in the middle indicates the full moon, and the crescent pattern on the left and right sides should indicate the last quarter and the first quarter moon. The shoulders and upper abdomen of each white-clothed pottery bowl are composed of three complete moon patterns.

As far as the sun pattern is concerned, it is more common in the upper abdomen of the white-clothed painted pottery bowl in the third period of the Yangshao Culture. The sun patterns are radiant and lifelike. Each white-clothed painted pottery bowl has 12 sun patterns painted on the upper abdomen, supposedly representing 12 months of the year.

As for the sun halo pattern, the white-clothed painted pottery bowl decorated with the sun halo pattern belongs to the third period of the Yangshao Culture. The sun halo pattern is composed of the sun pattern in the middle, three parallel arc patterns on the left and right sides of the sun pattern, the dot pattern and ray pattern, and crescent pattern on both sides of the ray pattern. The halo pattern reflects an atmospheric optical phenomenon commonly known as wind circle or rain circle.

The astronomical patterns embellished on the painted pottery of the Yangshao Culture in Dahe Village are not like simple decorative patterns. They appeared on the banks of the Yellow River 4,400-5,500 years ago. These astronomical images serve as the material testimony to the process of our ancestors' looking up at astronomy, exploring nature and making a dialogue with nature. The ancestors of Dahe Village who lived along the Yellow River tried to live and produce according to the changes in laws that were learned from observations about nature and the

月牙纹应该表示下弦月与上弦月。每件白衣彩陶钵的肩和上腹分别由三组完整的月亮纹构成。

就太阳纹而言，大河村彩陶的太阳纹多见于仰韶文化第三期白衣彩陶钵的上腹位置。太阳纹光芒四射，形象逼真，每件白衣彩陶钵的上腹都绘有 12 个太阳纹，应该是代表一年中有 12 个月份。

就日晕纹而言，饰有日晕纹的白衣彩陶钵属仰韶文化第三期。日晕纹图案由中部的太阳纹、太阳纹左右两侧三道平行弧线纹及其上、下的圆点纹、射线纹，以及射线纹两侧的月牙纹构成。日晕纹所反映的是一种被俗称为风圈或雨圈的大气光学现象。

大河村仰韶文化彩陶上所绘饰的天文图案，不太像是单纯的花纹装饰，它们出现在距今 4400—5500 年的黄河岸边，这些天文图像是我们祖先仰观天文，探索自然，与自然对话的物质见证。生活在大河上下的大河村先民试图通过对自然及宇宙世界的观察，来使自己的生产、生活也与自然规律的变化相一致。透过这些天文图像，我们看到了大河村先民经过漫长岁月积累起来的知识体系与丰富的精神世界。

2. 郑州大河村遗址经典建筑形制

大河村房屋建筑遗迹所展示的房屋建造技术被认为奠定了中国传统建筑的基础。大河村仰韶先民的房屋以地面建筑为主，平面有长方形或正方形，面积大小不等，但建筑方法多为木骨整塑陶房，其中以大河村仰韶文化第三期编号为 F1—F4 的房屋基址最有代表性（图 2-6）。

F1—F4 是一组东西并列的四间一体的连体建筑群，排列顺序由西向东依次编为 F2、F1、F3、F4，除 F4 为梯形外，其余均为长方形。发掘时这一组连体建筑距地表 1.8 米。该组建筑群的房门向南，位于 F2 南墙中部偏西，门宽 50 厘米。屋内东北角土台发掘时出土有一罐碳化粮食、两枚莲子和一块长约 50 厘米的木炭。除此之外，F2 中还出土有陶罐、陶壶、陶缸、砺石和陶弹丸等。

universe. Through these astronomical images, we can see the accumulation of knowledge and rich spiritual world of the ancestors of Dahe Village over the long years.

2. The Classic Architectural Form of Zhengzhou Dahe Village Site

It is believed that the house construction technology displayed in the building remains of Dahe Village has laid the foundation for traditional Chinese architecture. The houses of the Yangshao ancestors of Dahe Village are mainly ground buildings which take up rectangular or square areas, varying in size. They are often constructed with a wooden structure and mud walls and then fired in a pottery-making way. The construction method is called "mu gu zheng su" (wood-bone house) in Chinese. Among all those of the Yangshao Culture of Dahe Village, the building sites numbered F1-F4 of the third phase are the most representative ones (Fig. 2-6).

F1-F4 is a group of four-room conjoined buildings. And from west to east are F2, F1, F3, F4 respectively. Except for F4, which is trapezoidal, the rest are rectangular. When being excavated, this group of connected buildings was 1.8 meters above the ground. The door is in the west of the F2 south wall and faces south, with the width of 50 centimeters. A pot of carbonized grain, two lotus seeds, and a piece of charcoal about 50-centimeter-long were unearthed during excavations on the soil platform in the northeast corner of the house. In addition, objects like clay jars, clay pots, clay vats, ventifacts and pottery pellets were also unearthed in F2.

F1 lies between F2 and F3, separated from F2 by a wall, from which we may infer that they were constructed at the same time. A 3.7-meter-long partition wall is added in the room, which is from the south wall to the north, and turns eastward after that. The partition wall divides F1 into two parts: the outer room and the suite. And there used to be two doors in the F2 building. One was in the west of the north wall, facing north. The bottom of the 0.5-meter-wide door was made of fired clay into a threshold which was smeared with a layer of sandy fine silt on the surface. The other one was in the north of the east wall, facing east. But it can't be seen now because the expansion of F3 and F4 forced its closure, and another thin wall was built there. Inside F1, we can see one fire pit and two

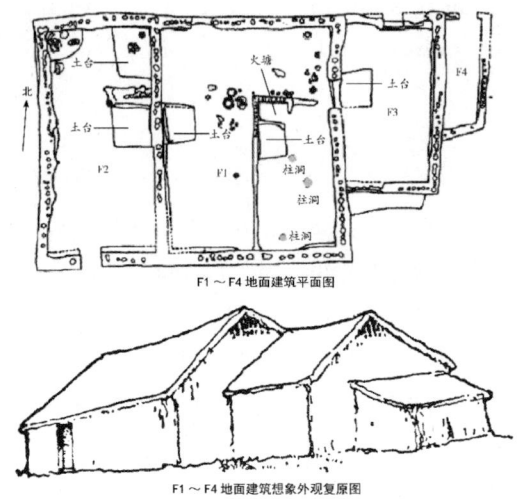

图 2-6　F1—F4 地面建筑平面和想象外观复原图
Fig. 2-6　F1–F4 restoration plan of ground building plane and imaginary appearance

F1 位于 F2 与 F3 之间，它与 F2 一墙之隔，应该是同时建筑的。房内由南墙往北加筑了一道南北长 3.7 米而后转向东拐的隔墙，隔墙将 F1 分成外间与套间两部分。F2 曾经有两个门，一个门位于北墙西部，门向北开，门宽 50 厘米，底部用红烧土块筑成一道门槛，门槛表面涂抹一层砂质细泥。另一个门位于东墙北部，向东开，东门在扩建 F3、F4 时封闭不用，并加筑薄墙一道。F1 内有土台两个，火塘一个。土台的修筑方法是先在地坪上用草拌泥土坯修砌，表面涂抹厚约 1 厘米的砂质细泥，并抹光。土台中部被烧成灰青，四周呈红色，并有多道龟裂缝。

F3、F4 位于 F1 的东侧，为二次扩建而成。F3 平面呈长方形，南北长 3.7 米，东西宽 2.1 米，房门向北设在北墙中部，门宽 50 厘米，底部用灰黏土筑有门槛，门槛高 10 厘米，宽 19 厘米。F4 位于 F3 东侧，平面呈梯形，房门向北，位于北墙中间。F4 面积较小，室内又有烟熏痕迹和灰烬，门外有大量木炭堆积，很可能是用来保留火种的。

F1—F4 房基内以 F1、F2 出土遗物最为丰富，其中陶器有鼎、罐、钵、

青海玛多县的黄河湿地 / 摄影/ 董保华
The Yellow River wetland in Maduo County, Qinghai Province (photo by Dong Baohua)

瓮、豆、瓶等 20 余件，还有陶纺轮、陶弹丸、骨镞、骨簪、砺石等遗物，著名的双连壶也出土于此处。考古工作者对 F2 木炭标本测年显示，F1—F4 的年代距今 5040±100 年。

大河村地面建筑的建筑方法始终采用"木骨整塑"的建筑工艺，这种工艺的特征是墙内布满柱洞、芦苇束和横木痕迹，而且整个房基均被烧成坚硬的砖红色，这样就使房屋具有坚固耐用、防潮保温的特点（图 2-7）。这种"木骨整塑"的建筑工序和施工方法，不仅为研究中国古代建筑的起源提供了罕见的佐证，也为研究我国家庭和私有制的起源提供了实物资料。

从李家沟、裴李岗，再到大河村，黄河文明的曙光穿越了晨曦的薄雾，即将在东亚大陆上闪耀灿烂的光芒！

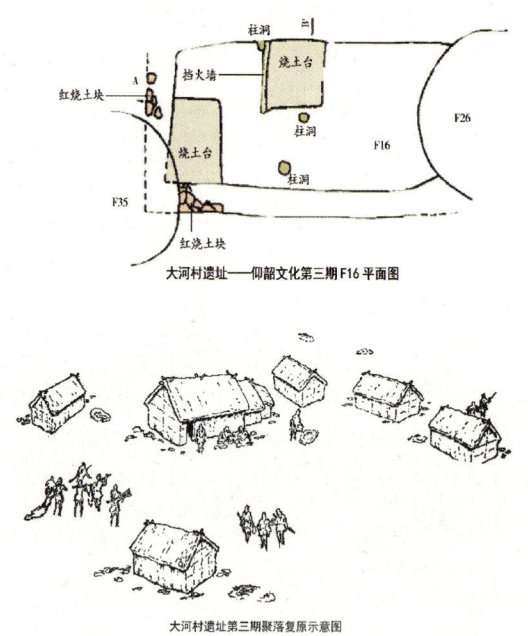

图 2-7　大河村遗址第三期建筑平面和聚落复原图

Fig. 2-7　Ground building plane plan and settlement restoration plan of the third phase of the Dahe Village Site

earthen platforms, the constructing method of which is to first repair the ground with grass-mixed mud adobe, smear the surface with about 1-centimeter-thick sandy fine silt, and polish it. The middle part of the earthen platform was burned to grayish blue, all around it being red with many cracks.

F3 and F4 are located on the east side of F1 and are constructed in the second expansion. The F3 plane is rectangular, 3.7 meters long from north to south and 2.1 meters wide from east to west. The door is in the middle of the north wall, facing north, and it is 50-centimeter-wide. The bottom is built with gray clay into a threshold that is 10-centimeter-high and 19-centimeter-wide. F4, located on the east of F3 with trapezoidal plane, has its door facing north in the middle of the north wall. The area of F4 is relatively small, with smoke traces and ashes inside, and a large amount of charcoal accumulation outside the door, which was probably used to keep the fire.

Among F1-F4, F1 and F2 are the most abundant in relics unearthed, including more than 20 pieces of pottery like tripods, jars, bowls, urns, compotes and bottles, as well as pottery spinning wheels, pottery pellets, bone arrowheads, bone hairpins, ventifacts and others. The famous twin pot was also unearthed here. Archaeologists have dated F2 charcoal specimens and found that the history of F1 to F4 can be traced back to 5040 ± 100 years ago.

The construction method always adopted for Dahe Village's ground buildings is "mu gu zheng su" (wood-bone house), which is characterized by the following: walls full of marks of column holes, reed bunches and beams, and the entire building foundation burnt hard and brick-red. Such buildings are solid, durable, damp-proof and warm (Fig. 2-7). The construction process and method of "mu gu zheng su" (wood-bone house) provide both rare evidence for the origin of ancient China's architecture and real materials for the study of the origin of Chinese family and private ownership.

From Lijiagou to Peiligang, and then to Dahe Village, the Yellow River civilization has shone through the mist of dawn, and is about to shine brightly over the entire East Asian Continent!

三、黄河大改道、大禹治水与国家的诞生

1. 史前时期黄河的改道

据地质学研究成果,距今115万年前的晚早更新世,黄河流域还未形成独立的内陆水系,但是随着青藏高原的逐渐抬升,在经历了中更新世之后,黄河上游的湖盆逐渐连通在一起,由此构成了黄河中、上游水系的基本轮廓;直至距今十万年至一万年间的晚更新世,黄河开始演变成为贯通海口的一条年轻内陆大河。黄河流经黄土高原,挟带的大量泥沙在进入下游平原后迅速沉积,以至于造成了黄河下游河道不断决溢和改变。

黄河河道变迁的范围大致在郑州以东,北抵天津,南达江淮,南北纵横约25万平方千米的区域之内。渤海、黄海海底的地质地貌调查结果显示,在渤海、黄海两大海域的海底居然可以发现多条古河道。以横贯北部和南部的大河道而言,这条大河道的起始端在今渤海湾西岸天津外海底,形成时间在距今70000—36000年和25000—10000年前,此时正是早、晚大理冰期,由于海平面下降,海底裸露成陆,黄河在此流入渤海,黄河所经之处,冲刷、下切形成了河道遗迹。无独有偶,在距今45000—25000年前的晚更新世的大理亚间冰期,黄河还曾取道淮河以北的今苏北一带,并由此流注南黄海。地质学家们推断黄河往返于渤海和南黄海之间,至少可追溯至晚更新世之际(图2-8)。

全新世以来的一万年间,发生在黄海、渤海之间的黄河改道,不仅扫荡了整个华北大平原,而且极大地影响了华夏文明的发展。大约在距今4000年或早于4000年前后,自由奔流的黄河摆过头来,由原来的走今淮北平原入海改道东北,再由河北平原重新流入渤海。这一漫长的过程正与中国古史上尧舜禹的时代相对应。而从考古学文化上来看,尧舜禹所处的距今4000年前后,正是考古学上所谓的龙山文化晚期,这一时期大洪水正肆虐整个东亚大陆。《孟子·滕文公上》说:"当尧之时,

III. The Great Diversion of the Yellow River, Dayu's Water Control and the Birth of the Country

1. Diversion of the Yellow River in Prehistoric Times

According to geological research results, in the late Early Pleistocene, 1.15 million years ago, the Yellow River Basin had not yet formed an independent inland water system. During the Middle Pleistocene, the basins were gradually connected together, constituting the basic outline of the middle and upper reaches of the Yellow River. Until the Late Pleistocene, 100,000 to 10,000 years ago, the Yellow River began to evolve as a young inland river that runs into the sea. The Yellow River flows through the Loess Plateau, and the large amount of sediment carried by it is quickly deposited after entering the lower plains, resulting in continuous flooding and diversions in the lower reaches of the Yellow River.

The scope of the Yellow River channel changes is roughly within an area of approximately 250,000 square kilometers, east to Zhengzhou, north to Tianjin, and south to Jianghuai. The geological and geomorphological surveys of the seabed of the Bohai Sea and the Yellow Sea show that many ancient river channels can be found in the seabed of the two. In terms of the large river channel that traverses the north and the south, the beginning of it is on the seafloor of the west coast of the Bohai Bay around Tianjin. It was formed during the periods of 70,000- 36,000 years ago and 25,000-10,000 years ago, which are the early and late "Dali Ice Age." At that time, due to the drop in sea level, the seabed was exposed as land, from which the Yellow River flowed into the Bohai Sea. Wherever the Yellow River passes, the relics are formed by scouring and eroding. Coincidentally, during the Late Pleistocene Dali subinterglacial period, which was 45,000-25,000 years ago, the Yellow River also passed through the north of the Huai River, the nowadays northern part of Jiangsu, and then flowed into the South Yellow Sea. Geologists infer that the Yellow River travels back and forth between the Bohai Sea and the South Yellow Sea at least as far back as the Late Pleistocene (Fig. 2-8).

In the 10,000 years since the Holocene, the diversion of the Yellow River between the Yellow Sea and the Bohai Sea not only swept the entire North China Plain, but also greatly affected the development of Chinese civilization. About

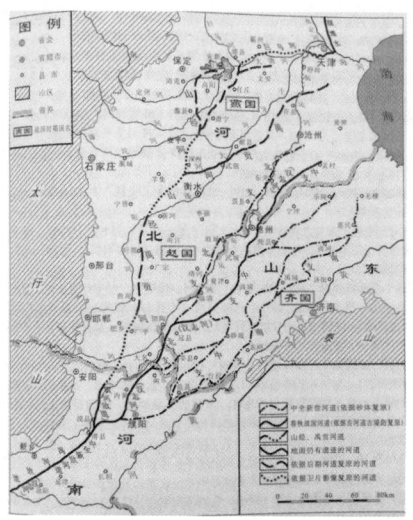

图 2-8　西汉以前黄河下游河道复原图
邹逸麟、张修桂主编：《中国历史自然地理》，科学出版社，2013。
Fig. 2-8　Restoration plan of the lower reaches of the Yellow River before the Western Han Dynasty
Edited by Zou Yilin and Zhang Xiugui: *Chinese History and Physical Geography*, Science Press, 2013.

天下洪水泛滥，在中原大地上，由于禽兽大量繁殖，五谷没有收成，飞禽走兽危害人类，到处都是它们的踪迹……大禹疏通黄河下游的九条河道，疏导济水、漯水，使九河、济、漯之水流入大海。大禹还把汝水、汉水进行了治理，疏通了淮水、泗水的淤塞之处，并使它们注入长江，除去了这些水灾，中原才可以生产。在这个时候，大禹在外治水八年（一说十三年），因为忙于疏导河川，三次路过家门都没有去探望家人。"

2. 大禹治水与黄河流域部落的凝聚整合

尧舜之际，黄河流域的先民们曾经花数十年的时间治理这次由黄河大改道引起的大洪水泛滥。先是禹的父亲——鲧，因"九载弗成"而被殛于羽山，鲧被杀之地羽山据说在山东南部郯城南境，考古学家多以此为黄河下游仍走淮北平原入海的证据。继承父业继续治水的大禹并未将

4,000 years ago or before, the free-running Yellow River changed its course from the Huaibei Plain to the northeast, and then re-flowed into the Bohai Sea from the Hebei Plain. This long process corresponds to the era of Yao, Shun and Yu in ancient Chinese history. From the perspective of archaeological culture, Yao, Shun, and Yu lived around 4,000 years ago, which was the so-called late Longshan Culture in archaeology. During this period, great floods were ravaging the entire East Asian Continent. According to *The Book of Master Meng*, "When Yao was in authority, flood overwhelmed the world. On the land of the Central Plains, due to the large multiplication of animals, there was little harvest of grains. Birds and beasts endangered humans, and their traces were everywhere ... Dayu worked with others to dredge the nine courses in the lower reaches of the Yellow River, and the Ji River and the Luo River, leading them to the sea. Dayu also improved the conditions of the Ru River and the Han River, and dredged the siltation of the Huai River and the Si River, which helped them flow into the Yangtze River and left the place safe from floods. Thus regular production can take place in the Central Plains. According to legend, Dayu did not return home to his family for eight (some say thirteen) years despite passing his house three times for water control work."

2. Dayu's Water Control and the Integration of Tribes in the Yellow River Basin

At the time of Yao and Shun, the ancestors in the Yellow River Basin spent decades controlling the flood caused by the great diversion of the Yellow River. First, Yu's father, Gun, was killed for "failure to control floods after nine years" in Yushan, which is said to be in the south of Tancheng in southern Shandong Province. Taking this as evidence, archaeologists insist that the lower Yellow River still enters the sea through the Huaibei Plain. Dayu, who followed in his father's footsteps and continued to control water, did not identify all the water systems here as single units. Instead, based on the knowledge of the natural geographical situation of the East Asian Continent, he suggested "the lower Yellow River flows through nine courses" and the conception materialized. Later generations of water specialists believed that this method of diverting flood water along the way was the key to the ultimate success of Dayu's water control.

水系归为一统,而是根据东亚大陆的自然地理形势,将黄河下游"播为九河",允许水分流入海。后世的水利学家都认为这种顺水势分流洪水的分水方法是大禹治水获得最终成功的关键。

在治水过程中,尧还让负责畜牧的益、管理农业的后稷、掌管教化百姓的契共同辅佐大禹。益、后稷、契是当时方国的首领,大禹不仅赢得了他们的信任与尊敬,还受到众多方国首领和百姓的拥戴。大禹带领大家在高处立起木杆作为标志,根据山川地形、地貌划定了九州的范围和界限,他们还按照河流的自然走向疏浚河道,并最终打通了黄河通往大海的水道。大禹为治理洪水劳身焦思,薄衣食、卑宫室,不敢有丝毫的松懈。为了了解各地治水情况,大禹陆行乘车、水行乘船、泥行乘橇、山行乘檋,常常左手拿着准绳、右手带着规矩,亲临各地督促施工。大禹的勘察与治水,不仅沟通了东亚大陆南北间氏族,也是对中华大地进行了一次大规模的调查和整治。

3. 最早国家——夏王朝(公元前 2070—前 1600 年)的诞生

治水活动,最终促成了统一国家——夏王朝的诞生。夏商周断代工程将夏王朝的纪年确定在公元前 21 世纪至前 17 世纪,基本年代框架估定为公元前 2070 年至公元前 1600 年,被岁月迷雾重重笼罩的夏王朝的历史开始变得清晰。

司马迁在《史记·夏本纪》中记载了夏王朝十四世十七王,其中的禹、启、太康、中康、相等四世五王都被认为是夏代早期的几位君王,与这一时期相对应的考古学文化主要是中原龙山文化晚期和新砦期遗存,作为这一时期代表性遗址的登封王城岗被考古学界认定为就是大禹的都城——禹都阳城。

1977 年,在登封王城岗考古学家发现了一座面积近一万平方米的小城,结合文献中"禹都阳城"的记载,大家倾向该城有可能就是大禹的都城——阳城。2002 年,在原来的小城以西,又发现一座带护城壕

Yao also asked the man in charge of animal husbandry, Yi, the man in charge of agriculture, Hou Ji, and the man in charge of education, Qi, to help Dayu. Yi, Hou Ji, and Qi were the heads of the tribal alliance at that time. Dayu not only won their trust and respect, but also received the support from many tribal alliance leaders and people. Dayu led everyone to erect wooden poles at high places as a sign, and identified the scopes and boundaries of Nine Provinces of China based on the topography of mountains and rivers. They also dredged the Yellow River according to the natural direction of it, and finally opened up the waterway from the Yellow River to the sea. Dayu struggled to control the flood, and he did not dare to relax in the slightest. In order to have a general understanding of the water control conditions in various places, Dayu traveled by cart on land, boat in water, sled in mud, and sedan chair in mountains. He often personally came to the places under construction for supervision, with a plumb line in his left hand and rulers in his right hand. Dayu's job of exploration and water control not only enhanced the communication of clans from the north and south of East Asia, but also conducted a large-scale investigation and regulation of the ancient China's land.

3. The Earliest Country—the Birth of the Xia Dynasty (2070-1600 BC)

Water control activities eventually led to the birth of a unified country—the Xia Dynasty. The Xia-Shang-Zhou Chronology Project dated the span of the Xia Dynasty at between the 21st century BC and the 17th century BC, and the basic chronology was estimated to be from 2070 BC to 1600 BC. The history of the Xia Dynasty, which was shrouded in years of mist, started to be clarified.

Sima Qian recorded seventeen kings of fourteen reigns in *The Historical Records*. Among them, the five kings like Yu, Qi, Taikang, Zhongkang and Xiang were considered to be the early kings of the Xia Dynasty. The archaeological culture corresponding to this period is mainly the remains of the late Longshan Culture of the Central Plains and the Xinzhai Period. As a representative site of this period, Dengfeng Wangchenggang is recognized by the archaeological world as the capital of Dayu—Yudu Yangcheng.

In 1977, archaeologists discovered a small town with an area of nearly 10,000 square meters at the Wangchenggang Site in Dengfeng. Based on the records of "Yudu Yangcheng" in the literature, they tended to believe that this city might

的龙山文化晚期的大型城址。大城总面积可达 34.8 万平方米，城中发现了大面积夯土遗迹、白陶器、玉石琮、祭祀坑等。王城岗龙山晚期大、小城址的建筑年代大致同时，小城原为大城的一部分（图 2-9）。考古学者们认为登封王城岗大、小古城址位于禹都阳城的旧址范围之内，小城很可能是禹都的宗庙遗迹，而小城内"奠基坑"则很可能就是祭祀坑的遗存。大城有长达数百米的南城壕，这段城壕与地表高差有 4 米多，但其底部高差却不超过 0.4 米，这一高一低之间显示出筑建古阳城的先人们已经掌握了相当的测量技术与水平挖掘技术，文献中讲大禹治水时常常"左准绳、右规矩"很可能就是指此种技术。考古学家还通过模拟实验，推测了建筑这座大城所需的工程量，如果用 1000 个青壮劳动力每天工作 8 小时，需要连续工作 1 年零 2 个月，如果再加上测量、规划、管理、监督、工具及后勤保障人员，那么这一宏大工程远非王城岗聚落本身所能提供。以王城岗为中心，必然存在着一个数量众多、范围广大、内部社会结构复杂的聚落群，以王城岗遗址为中心的整个聚落群体共同完成了这座龙山晚期古城的建筑。

透过王城岗遗址，我们隐约地看到了生长在黄河岸边的中国早期国家的雏形，她正从历史深处向我们走来。

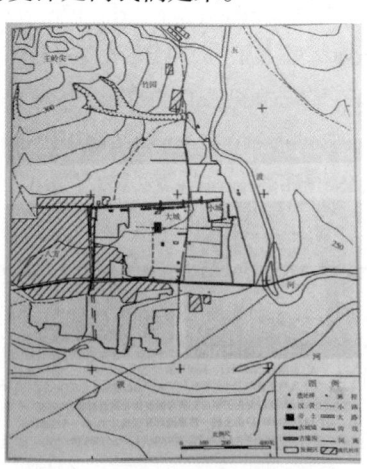

图 2-9 王城岗大小城址关系与平面

Fig. 2-9 Locational plan of the large and small cities of Wangchenggang

be the capital of Dayu—Yangcheng. In 2002, to the west of the former small town, another large-scale city site with a moat from the late Longshan Culture was discovered. The total area of the big city covers 348,000 square meters, and large areas of rammed earth relics, white pottery, jade cong, and sacrificial pits have been found there. The large and small cities of late Longshan Culture Period found at the Wangchenggang Site were built in the same period and were the two different parts of one building (Fig. 2-9). Archaeologists supposed that the site of the two ancient cities was located within the scope of the former site of Yudu Yangcheng. The small town was likely to be the ruins of the ancestral temple of Yudu, while the "memorial pit" in the small town was probably the remains of the sacrificial pit. The hundreds of meters long south moat surrounding the large city had a difference of elevation of more than 4 meters from the ground, but the elevation difference at the bottom was not more than 0.4 meter. It showed that the ancestors who built the ancient Yangcheng had mastered considerable level of measurement and horizontal excavation technology. According to the literature, Dayu often held "a plumb line in the left hand and a ruler and a torque in the right" when taming the floods, which probably referred to the above-mentioned technology. Archaeologists also speculated on the amount of work needed to build this big city through simulation experiments. If 1,000 young laborers work 8 hours a day, they need to work continuously for 1 year and 2 months to complete the city. If surveying, planning, management, supervision, tools and logistic support personnel were also included, then this grand project would be far beyond what Wangchenggang settlement itself could provide. Centering on Wangchenggang, there must be a large number of settlements with a large scope and complex internal social structure, and they jointly completed the construction of this ancient city in the late Longshan Period.

We can see the embryonic form of China's early state growing along the Yellow River through the Wangchenggang Site. Early China is coming towards us from the depth of history.

第三章

根与魂：黄河当中流

Chapter 3

Root and Soul: the Yellow River Flowing in the Middle

　　黄河文化发源自黄河中下游地区，以河洛盆地为核心的中原地区是历史上黄河文化的根魂所在。中原地区的黄河文化起源早、成熟快，具有强大的传播、同化能力，在先秦、秦汉直至唐宋时期一直是华夏文明的典型代表，产生了灿若群星的物质文化和精神文明成果，持续向周边地区以及域外国家辐射出耀眼的光芒，宛若滚滚黄河之中流砥柱，撑起中华民族的精神脊梁，成为历代中华儿女共同的精神归宿和民族凝聚力源泉。

一、寻根往河洛：老家河南的向往

1. 婚姻制度起源

　　中国史前部落联盟时代，已经初步形成了早期国家的雏形，即古史所称的"三皇五帝"时代。司马迁《史记》中把黄帝、颛顼、帝喾、尧、舜合称"五帝"，作《五帝本纪》列为篇首，现代研究亦证明了"五帝时代"记载的可靠性。而更早的"三皇"——伏羲氏、燧人氏、神农氏则属于传闻，但通过近期史前考古学资料的证明，文献中所说的"三皇"虽然不能以具体的人物视之，但其所代表的时代应该是中华民族早期不同历史阶段的代名词。伏羲氏开启的三皇时代与后来的黄帝时代交织在一起，成为华夏民族形成的两大制度，伏羲氏亦被亿万华人尊称为中华人文始祖。

　　伏羲氏又称太昊伏羲氏，与少昊族同为中国上古时代东夷集团前后相继的两大氏族，分布在今豫西、鲁东的黄河下游地区。古代文献记载伏羲以陈为都并葬于此，在今河南省淮阳县。纪念伏羲的太昊陵春秋时期已建，历代均有修葺，经年祭祀不绝。今淮阳县现存陵园占地500余亩，殿宇巍峨，濒蔡河之滨，临万顷碧波，甚为壮观，号称天下第一陵（图3-1）。

The Yellow River culture originated in the middle and lower reaches of the Yellow River, and the Central Plains with the Heluo Basin as the core was the root of the Yellow River culture in history. The Yellow River culture in the Central Plains appeared early and developed quickly with powerful dissemination and assimilation. As a typical representative of Chinese civilization from pre-Qin, the Qin and Han dynasties to the Tang and Song dynasties, it produced brilliant achievements of material culture and spiritual civilization, which influenced surrounding areas and countries continuously. Like the mainstay of the Yellow River, it supports the spiritual backbone of the Chinese nation, and becomes the common spiritual home and the source of national cohesion for Chinese descendants.

Ⅰ. Finding Roots in Heluo Basin: the Yearning of Our Hometown in Henan

1. The Origin of the Marriage System

In prehistoric tribal alliance period, the early state took shape in China, namely the era of "the Three Sovereigns and Five Emperors" in ancient history. In Sima Qian's book *The Historical Records*, Huangdi, Zhuanxu, Diku, Yao, and Shun are collectively referred to as the "Five Emperors," and "The Biographic Sketches of the Five Emperors" is listed at the beginning of the book. Modern research has also proved the reliability of the records of the "Five Emperors Era." The earlier "Three Sovereigns"—Fuxi, Suiren, and Shennong are tales, but according to recent prehistoric archaeological data, the era they represent should be synonymous with the different historical stages of the early Chinese nation even if the "Three Sovereigns" mentioned in the literature cannot be regarded as specific characters. The era of the "Three Sovereigns" initiated by Fuxi and later Huangdi era are intertwined and become the two major systems to form Chinese nation. Fuxi is thus revered as the ancestor of the Chinese humanistic culture by hundreds of millions of Chinese.

山东阳谷陶城铺闸 摄影/董保华
The floodgate in Taochengpu Village, Yanggu County, Shandong Province (photo by Dong Baohua)

图 3-1　淮阳伏羲太昊陵

Fig.3-1　Fuxi Taihao Mausoleum in Huaiyang County

太昊伏羲氏为中国古代文明做出了许多贡献，其中最重要的就是制嫁娶、正姓氏，制定了影响后世深远的婚姻制度。伏羲以前，人们过着近亲通婚的血缘婚姻生活。伏羲时代的人们已经认识到近亲通婚的危害，改革婚姻制度，伏羲氏应该是最早实行族外婚姻的部族。这是人类婚姻制度的重大进步，随之而来的是实行（族外）对偶婚和个体婚（一夫一妻制）。而婚姻制度的变化是中国姓氏制度产生的直接原因，因为族外婚必须至少有两个部族，而原始氏族之间区别不同血缘关系的唯一因素，就是他们源自不同的始祖先，这位始祖先就成为他们氏族存在的标志和姓氏。

在中原大地上广泛流传的有关伏羲的神话（图 3-2），从一个侧面印证了河南是中华姓氏起源地的史实，中华民族婚姻发展史上的族外婚以及与之有密切联系的姓氏制度都首创于河南。

Fuxi Clan, also known as Taihao Fuxi Clan, along with Shaohao Clan, were two successive clans of the Dongyi Group in ancient China, and lived in the lower reaches of the Yellow River in present western Henan and eastern Shandong. Ancient documents recorded that Fuxi took Chen, today's Huaiyang County, Henan Province, as the capital and was buried here. The Taihao Mausoleum to commemorate Fuxi was built during the Spring and Autumn Period, being repaired throughout the ages, with ceaseless sacrifice ceremonies over the years. Today, the existing Mausoleum in Huaiyang County covers an area of more than 500 mu, equal to 82 acres, with majestic palaces close to the Cai River, and surrounded by thousands of hectares of blue waves. Taihao Mausoleum is so spectacular that it is known as the world's first tomb (Fig.3-1).

Taihao Fuxi made many contributions to ancient Chinese civilization, and the most important of which were the establishment of marriages, surnames, and the formulation of a marriage system that had a profound impact on future generations. Before it, people lived in groups with consanguineous marriage. In the Fuxi era, people realized the harm of consanguineous marriage and reformed the marriage system. The Fuxi Clan may be the first tribe to practice extra-clan marriage, which is a major advancement in the human marriage system, followed by the implementation of (extra-clan) pairing marriage and individual marriage (monogamy). The change of the marriage system is the direct cause of the Chinese surname system, because there must be at least two clans in ex-clan marriage, and the only factor to distinguish different blood relations among primitive clans is that they originate from different ancestors, who become the symbols and surnames of their clans.

The myths about Fuxi that spread widely in the Central Plains confirm the historical facts from one side that Henan is the origin of Chinese surnames (Fig.3-2), and the extra-clan marriage in the history of Chinese marriage and the relevant surname system are also first created in Henan.

图 3-2 宋代画家马麟笔下的伏羲

Fig.3-2 Fuxi in the works of Ma Lin who was an artist in the Song Dynasty

2. 中华姓氏

以河洛文化为代表的中原文化是中华民族的精神家园，河南则是中华姓氏的根柢所在。河南姓氏文化资源在全国首屈一指，是海内外华人寻根祭祖情怀的重要寄托。"寻根到中原，河洛是故乡""豫见中原，老家河南"等温情话语，亲切地展现了河南在中华姓氏文化中的独特地位。

有学者统计，当今中国 100 大姓中，有 80 余姓源于河南或其起源与河南密切相关。李、王、张、刘、陈前五大姓中，李、张、陈均出自河南，王姓最早的一支及刘姓最主要的源头也都在河南。其后的杨、赵、

2. The Root of Chinese Surnames

The Central Plains Culture represented by the Heluo Culture is the spiritual home of the Chinese nation, and Henan is the root of the Chinese surname. Serving as the important sustenance of Chinese people at home and abroad who want to seek roots and worship their ancestors, the cultural resources of surnames in Henan are second to none in China. "Looking for the roots in the Central Plains, we find Heluo is the hometown," "Meeting in the Central Plains, we are back home to Henan" and other warm words cordially demonstrate Henan's unique status in the Chinese surname culture.

According to the statistics of some scholars, more than 80 of the 100 major surnames in China originate from Henan or their origin is closely related to Henan. Among the top 5 surnames of Li, Wang, Zhang, Liu and Chen, Li, Zhang and Chen are all from Henan. The earliest branch of Wang and the most important source of Liu are also in Henan. Among the following 14 surnames, including Yang, Zhao, Huang, Zhou, Wu, Xu, Sun, Hu, Zhu, Gao, Lin, He, Guo and Ma, 10 of them originate from Henan, or one of their branches originate from Henan. The total population of these 19 major surnames accounts for about 55% of the Han population in China. It can be said that more than half of the Han compatriots in China today have their ancestral roots in today's Henan Province.

Henan is also the source of most Chinese surnames in Hong Kong, Taiwan and overseas countries. In the long history, many ancestors from Henan carried the advanced culture and technology of the Central Plains and went on moving south to Fujian, Guangdong, Taiwan and Southeast Asia (Fig.3-3). The ancestors of the four surnames "Chen, Lin, Huang, and Zheng" in Taiwan today are said to "be in Fujian five hundred years ago, and in Henan a thousand years ago." The large numbers of overseas Chinese living in Southeast Asia are mostly descendants of the Hakka people in Guangdong and Fujian, and most of their ancestors come from Henan.

黄、周、吴、徐、孙、胡、朱、高、林、何、郭、马14姓,有10姓源于河南或有一支源头在河南。这19个大姓总人口约占国内汉族人口的55%,可以说,当今国内半数以上汉族同胞的祖根都在今河南。

河南亦是当今多数港台及海外华人姓氏源头地,在悠久的历史长河中,众多河南先民携带中原地区先进的文化和技术,持续南迁闽、粤,流播台湾及东南亚地区(图3-3)。当今台湾地区的"陈、林、黄、郑"四大姓氏先祖,有"五百年前在福建,一千年前在河南"之说。而人数众多的东南亚华侨,多为广东、福建一带客家人后裔,其先祖亦多源自河南。

图 3-3 福建泉州河洛移民命名的洛阳江和洛阳桥（始建于北宋）
Fig.3-3 The Luoyang River and Luoyang Bridge (built in the Northern Song Dynasty) named by the Heluo immigrants in Quanzhou, Fujian

二、铸魂在中原：文明成就的核心

1. 不断创造革新的科学技术

从秦汉至唐宋时期，黄河中下游地区一直是中国的经济重心所在。农业作为历代封建王朝的立国之本尤其受到统治者的高度重视，以中原地区为核心的黄淮平原的农业技术有了突飞猛进的发展，大量土地得到进一步开发利用，水利工程逐步完善。而农业的繁荣和粮食产量的提高直接促进了城市的兴起和手工业的发展，使得社会物质财富得到不断的积累，长期占据世界领先的地位。

（1）农业生产

现代研究表明，中国的农业生产工具，殷商为铜、石并用时代，西周和春秋为铜、铁并用时代，战国以后则是铁器时代。文献及考古资料证实黄河流域农业生产工具成熟甚早，在商周时代，耒耜（耕地工具）、钱（锹铲类挖掘工具）、镈（锄草类工具）、铚（短镰类收割工具）、艾（剪刀式收割工具）等组合农具已经得到普遍应用，而渔猎工具如网、弓类亦种类繁多。秦汉以来，在黄河流域的中原地区，铁质农具得到普遍的使用，在性能上大大超过前代。如犁铧和犁壁已基本定型，构成近代犁的基本特征；牛耕技术得到推广，轻便高效的耧车的发明，大大提高了播种效率；东汉末年，中原地区还出现了可连续进行中耕除草的新式农具——"耪犁"。因此可以说，现代"耕耘"技术的源头产生在中原地区。

伴随着农业工具技术的发展，精耕细作技术在中原地区也有飞速的发展，在反映东汉时期洛阳地区农业情况的《四民月令》一书中有突出的体现，如适时、因时、因土耕作等原则，及时翻土磨压、保墒等抗旱技术。而采取垄沟互换、轮流耕作的"代田法"得以推广，极大地提高了农作物成活率和单位面积产量。2003 年考古工作者在河南内黄县三

II. Soul-casting in the Central Plains: Core of Civilization Achievements

1. Carrying on Innovation of Science and Technology

From the Qin and Han to the Tang and Song dynasties, the economic focus of China was always in the middle and lower reaches of the Yellow River. Agriculture—the very foundation of the feudal dynasties, was highly valued by its rulers. The agricultural technology of the Huang-Huai Plain, with the Central Plains as its core, improved by leaps and bounds. A large amount of land was further developed and utilized, and water conservancy projects gradually improved. The boom of agriculture and the boosting of grain output directly promoted the rise of cities and the development of handicraft industry, enabling social material wealth to accumulate continuously and take the lead in the world for a long time.

(1) Agricultural Production

Modern research shows that tools for agricultural production in China used to be made of bronze and stone in the Shang Dynasty, while bronze and iron were used in the Western Zhou Dynasty and the Spring and Autumn Period. After the Warring States Period, they were made of iron. Documentary and archaeological data confirm that agricultural production tools in the Yellow River Basin attained maturity very early. During the Shang and Zhou dynasties, a combination of farming tools was widely used—Leisi (a farming tool), Jian (a digging tool like a spade or shovel), Bo (a weeding tool), Zhi (a harvesting tool like a short sickle), and Yi (a harvesting tool like scissors) while fishing and hunting tools such as net and bow also varied. Since the Qin and Han dynasties, iron tools were widely used in the Central Plains of the Yellow River Basin, surpassing those of the previous dynasties. For example, ploughshares and plough moldboards practically took the shape, showing the essential characteristics of modern ploughs. The technology of cattle-farming plough was well advanced, and the invention of an animal-drawn seed plough, light and highly efficient, improved sowing efficiency greatly. At the end of the Eastern Han Dynasty, "Yunli" (a weeding plough)—a new type of agricultural tool for sustained weeding, appeared in the Central Plains. Therefore,

杨庄汉代聚落遗址清理出大片排列整齐、沟垄明晰的田垄遗址，作为目前国内发现的唯一汉代农田遗址，为我们真正理解汉代代田法在黄河流域的推广提供了真实的考古样本（图3-4）。

图 3-4　河南省内黄县三杨庄汉代聚落遗址出土之石磨
《河南内黄三杨庄汉代聚落遗址第二处庭院发掘简报》，《华夏考古》2010 年第 3 期
Fig.3-4　Stone mill unearthed at the Han Dynasty Settlement Site at Sanyangzhuang in Neihuang County of Henan Province
"Brief Report on Excavation of the Second Courtyard of the Han Dynasty Settlement Site at Sanyangzhuang in Neihuang County of Henan Province," 3rd issue of *Huaxia Archaeology*, 2010

（2）水利工程

中国最早的国家——夏王朝的诞生，与大禹治水过程中充分调动社会力量、整合华夏部族联盟有着密切的关系。此后以黄河流域为核心的历代封建王朝，推行以农为本的治国思想，十分重视农田水利建设，利用大一统集权帝国的力量优势，开展大规模的治理河流、营建水利活动，水利工程技术也得以不断积累进步，达到十分先进的水平。

东汉明帝时期王景治河，采用"堰流法"，根据黄河中下游荥阳至千乘海口（今山东境内）的地势情况，采取裁直河道以提高流速、设立水门以调节水势、沿堤筑坝以防止漫流、疏导与堵截相结合的高超技术，

there is good reason to say that modern "cultivation" technology originates in the Central Plains.

With the improvement of agricultural tool technology, intensive cultivation techniques also developed rapidly in the Central Plains. The principles of being in good time, adjusting measures to timing, and adjusting farming measures to soil, as well as drought resistance techniques—timely soil turning-over, soil grinding-and-covering, and soil moisture conservation were highlighted in the book *Simin Yueling* (*Monthly Agricultural Activities*), which reflected agricultural circumstances around Luoyang during the Eastern Han Dynasty. Meanwhile, "Substitution Method"—ditch swap and crop rotation, was popularized, greatly improving the survival rate of crops and the per unit yield. In 2003, at Sanyangzhuang in Neihuang County of Henan Province, archaeologists cleaned up large patches of farming sites, making neat and clear furrow ridge of the Han Dynasty settlement visible. As the only farming site of the Han Dynasty unearthed in China today, it provides real archeological samples for us to understand the spreading of Substitution Method in the Yellow River Basin (Fig.3-4).

(2) Water Conservancy Projects

The birth of the Xia Dynasty—the earliest kingdom in China, was closely related to the full mobilization of social forces and the integration of Huaxia tribal alliances in Dayu's flood control. Since then, the feudal dynasties with the Yellow River Basin as the core pursued agriculture-oriented governance ideology, attached great importance to the construction of irrigation and water conservancy, and took advantage of the strong power of the unified centralized kingdom to carry out large-scale river control and water conservancy construction. In this way, the water conservancy engineering technology got sustained development and reached a quite advanced level.

During the reign of Emperor Mingdi of the Eastern Han Dynasty, based on the terrain of Xingyang to Qiansheng Haikou (in today's Shandong Province) of the middle and lower reaches of the Yellow River, Wang Jing adopted "Weir Flow Method" to control it—cutting into straight channels to accelerate the flow rate, setting up water gates to regulate water potential, building dams along the embankments to prevent overflow, and combining dredging with blocking up, which became the model strategies for controlling the Yellow River later.

成为后世治理黄河的典范策略。

除了举世闻名的关中郑国渠、蜀地都江堰，秦朝时期在今河南济源市五龙口镇沁河出山口修建的引沁水灌溉枢纽工程，亦堪称典范，是中国最古老的水利工程之一。其渠首以枋木垒砌而成，故称"枋口"或"秦渠"，后改为石门筑造，历代增修扩建，唐代时可灌溉下游农田5万余亩。明万历年间自渠首扩建成五条主灌渠，形成"五龙"分水之势，统称五龙口（图3-5）。延续至新中国成立初期，其灌溉面积达到55万亩之多。其在地质勘探、分水冲沙、穿山凿洞、高程测量等科技运用方面达到了很高的技术水平。

秦汉至唐宋时期，中原地区修建了大量井灌、水渠和陂塘等水利设施，逐步形成了成体系的密集农业灌溉区域，大大促进了农业生产水平的提高，为历代集权中央王朝的政治稳定提供了充足的经济保障，也为中原文化长期在中国核心地位的确立奠定了坚实的物质基础。

（3）金属冶炼

黄河流域金属冶炼技术以冶铁技术为代表，在汉代以后得到突飞猛进的发展，广泛应用在农业、交通工具、兵器、建筑构件、生活用品铸造等领域，有力地促进了社会生产力的提高。而中原地区由于地处水陆要冲，交通便利，农商发达，矿产资源丰富，冶铁技术在古代中国长期处于领先地位。河南郑州古荥、巩县（今巩义市）铁生沟、南阳瓦房店发现的汉代冶铁遗址就是突出的代表。郑州古荥遗址出土了迄今国内发现最大的一座汉代冶铁炉，炉底面积8.5平方米，炉高5米以上，估算日产生铁可达1吨左右，可见其规模和产量之大（图3-6）。巩县铁生沟遗址总面积达2.1万平方米，发现有大量矿石加工厂、炼铁炉、熔炉、锻炉、炒钢炉、淬火坑、贮藏室等完整冶铁生产线遗址。而南阳瓦房店铸铁遗址规模更大，面积达12万平方米，延续时间更长，从西汉至东汉时期长达300余年薪火不绝。

从两汉至隋唐时期，中原地区的冶炼技术一直得到持续发展，如鼓

In addition to the world-famous Zhengguoqu (Zhengguo Canal Irrigation System) in Guanzhong (today's middle part of Shaanxi Province) and Dujiangyan (Dujiangyan Irrigation System) in Shudi (today's Sichuan Province), the Qinhe Irrigation Hub, built in the mountain pass at Wulongkou Town in Jiyuan City of Henan Province during the Qin Dynasty, is a model project and one of the oldest hydraulic engineering in China. The head of the Qinhe Irrigation Hub was first built up by Fangmu (timbers formed by cutting lengthwise along the wood), so it was called "Fangkou" or "Qin Canal." Later, it was rebuilt of stones and got expanded in successive dynasties. In the Tang Dynasty, it could irrigate more than 50,000 mu (equal to 8237 acres) of farmland. During the reign of Emperor Wanli in the Ming Dynasty, five main irrigation canals were extended from the head of the Qinhe Irrigation Hub, making the form of "Five Dragons" dividing water, collectively known as Wulongkou (Five Dragons' Mouths) (Fig. 3-5). Until the early days of new China, the Qin Canal reached a very high level in geological exploration, water diversion and sand sluicing, mountain tunneling, and height

图 3-5 河南省济源市五龙口水利设施——古广济渠首正面
Fig. 3-5 The front of the ancient Guangji Canal head — "Five Dragons' Mouths" water conservancy facilities at Jiyuan City of Henan Province

风技术、炒钢法、灌钢法与铸铁脱碳技术的革新应用,处于世界领先水平。金属制品的应用范围越来越广,在产量上亦达到了惊人规模,如唐代女皇武则天于证圣元年(695年),在东都洛阳城端门广场铸造的巨型"天枢"铜铁塔柱,高50余米,基座周长将近60米,使用铜铁高达200万斤,可见当时冶炼、铸造技术的发达和金属产量之巨大。

图 3-6　河南郑州古荥汉代冶铁遗址

Fig. 3-6　Iron-smelting remains of the Han Dynasty at Guxing in Zhengzhou of Henan Province

(4)陶瓷制造

古代中国以瓷器制品享誉世界,而瓷器脱胎于陶器制品工艺的不断进步。从史前时期直至北宋,地处黄河中下游的中原地区陶瓷制造技术以其工艺精良、高雅秀丽的特点长期引领时代风潮。公元前5000—3000年位于黄河中游的仰韶文化即以其色彩斑斓的彩陶制品令世人惊叹不已,地处河南省渑池县的仰韶村文化遗址亦因此惊艳世界。至秦汉时期,陶器制品的应用愈加普遍,在生活、建筑用品中广泛使用,施釉技术也更加成熟,至魏晋南北朝时期,早期瓷器在黄河流域已经出现。唐宋时期,瓷器制造技艺日趋成熟,逐渐达到工艺技术和审美艺术相结合的巅

measurement, with the irrigated area amounting to 550,000 mu (equal to 90,610 acres).

From the Qin and Han to the Tang and Song dynasties, a large number of water conservancy facilities were constructed in the Central Plains, such as well irrigation, canals and impounding reservoirs, gradually developing into a system of intensive agricultural irrigation areas. They greatly improved agricultural production, safeguarded sufficient economy for the political stability of successive centralized dynasties, and laid a solid material foundation for the establishment of the core position of Central Plains culture in China for a long time.

(3) Metal Smelting

The metal smelting technology in the Yellow River Basin represented by iron-smelting made a fantastic spurt after the Han Dynasty, which was widely used in agriculture, vehicles, weapons, building components, and casting of living articles, and promoted the social productivity effectively. Due to convenient transportation, well-developed agriculture and commerce, and abundant mineral resources, the iron-smelting technology in the Central Plains was in a leading position for a long time in ancient China. Prominent representatives are the Han Dynasty remains unearthed at Guxing of Zhengzhou, Tieshenggou of Gongxian (today's Gongyi City), and Wafangdian of Nanyang, all in Henan Province. The biggest Han Dynasty iron-smelting furnace ever found in China was excavated from the ancient Guxing ruins in Zhengzhou, which was more than 5 meters high, with 8.5-square-meter hearth area (Fig. 3-6). The production of raw iron was in such a large scale that it could have an estimated 1 ton daily. The iron-smelting remains at Tieshenggou of Gongxian were found to be a complete iron-smelting production line—a large number of mineral processing plants, blooming furnaces, smelters, forge furnaces, wrought steel furnaces, quenching pits, storage rooms and others, with a total area of 21,000 square meters. While Wafangdian iron-casting remains in Nanyang were even larger in scale, covering an area of 120,000 square meters and lasting without cease for more than 300 years from the Western Han Dynasty to the Eastern Han Dynasty.

From the Han to Sui and Tang dynasties, the smelting technology in the Central Plains took the lead in the world in the constant development of innovation in blast blowing technology, wrought steel method, pouring steel

峰，中原地区产出的唐三彩和宋钧瓷、汝瓷等即是其杰出代表作品。

唐三彩是唐代陶瓷的代表作品，以其色彩艳丽、造型生动而闻名，以黄、绿、白三色为主，故称"唐三彩"。因唐三彩最早、最多出土于洛阳，亦有"洛阳唐三彩"之称。现存河南巩义的唐三彩官窑遗址，是国内发现最早的专门烧制唐三彩的唐代官窑遗址群，也是唐代青白瓷、三彩瓷器的主要产地之一。遗址位于今巩义市东站镇黄冶河两岸（大、小黄冶村），出土唐三彩种类丰富，以生活用具和明器占多数，其中有三足炉、碗、盆、壶、罐、盂、杯、酒壶、酒盅等生活器具。

宋代官窑瓷器以"汝、官、钧、哥、定"五大名瓷并称，其中汝瓷和钧瓷的产地分别在今河南的汝州和禹州。汝瓷盛名于北宋，位列五大名瓷之首，以纯净温润的釉面，呈现出古玉般的内蕴光泽，反映出中国传统士大夫阶层清淡高雅的独特审美情趣（图3-7）。钧瓷以其独特釉料产生的神奇窑变而闻名于世，"入窑一色，出窑万彩"，钧瓷充满个性、变化万端、流光溢彩的艺术美感，受到后世收藏家的特殊青睐，民间历来有"家有万贯，不如钧瓷一片"之说，可见钧瓷之高超艺术成就。

图3-7 北宋汝窑三足奁（故宫博物院藏）

Fig. 3-7 Three-legged mirror case of Ru porcelain in the Northern Song Dynasty (collected in the Palace Museum)

method and decarbonization technology of cast iron. Metal wares were popular in application, with an amazing scale of output. For example, in the first year of Zhengsheng by the Empress Wu Zetian of the Tang Dynasty (695 AD), a huge copper and iron pylon pillar "Tianshu" was cast at Duanmen Square of Luoyang (used to be called the Eastern Capital of the Tang Dynasty). It was at a height of more than 50 meters and a foundation support circumference of nearly 60 meters, consuming copper and iron up to 2 million jin (equal to 1 million kilograms), which showed the advanced smelting and casting technology and huge metal output at that time.

(4) Ceramics Production

Ancient China had a great reputation in its porcelains, and porcelain grew out of the sustained progress of pottery craft. From the prehistoric period to the Northern Song Dynasty, the ceramic technology in the Central Plains of the middle and lower reaches of the Yellow River maintained leading the trend for a long time with its excellent craftsmanship and elegant beauty. Located in the middle reaches of the Yellow River from 5,000 BC to 3,000 BC, Yangshao Culture stunned the world with its colorful and gorgeous pottery wares, making Yangshao Village cultural site in Mianchi County of Henan Province star-struck in the world. Until the Qin and Han dynasties, the application of pottery became more and more common, widely used in daily life and architectural supplies, and the glazing technique grew more mature. By the Wei, Jin and Southern & Northern dynasties, early porcelain appeared in the Yellow River Basin. During the Tang and Song dynasties, porcelain making became more and more mature, gradually reaching the peak of combination of technical skills and aesthetic art. Tang tri-coloured pottery, and Jun porcelain and Ru porcelain of the Song Dynasty produced in the Central Plains were their outstanding representative works.

Tri-coloured pottery was a model of ceramics made in the Tang Dynasty, famous for its beautiful colours and lively design, mainly in the three colours of yellow, green and white, thus got its name of "Tang tri-coloured pottery." Because it was first and most unearthed in Luoyang, Tang tri-coloured pottery was also called "Luoyang Tang tri-coloured pottery." The existing ruins in Gongyi of Henan Province were the earliest official kilns of the Tang Dynasty ever found in

（5）天文历法

中国古代先民对天文观测、历法制定极为重视，一方面源自于先秦以来统治阶层对"天"的绝对敬仰，另一方面源自于区分节候、预测天象以指导农业生产的迫切现实需要。作为中国早期王朝政治核心区和农业起源地，黄河中下游地区亦是中国天文、历法成就最早的诞生地，并在秦汉、隋唐时期取得了突出的成就。

现存的河南偃师县东汉灵台遗址，是中国发现最早的大型天文台遗址，亦是展现中国古代天文学杰出成就的标志性建筑遗址。遗址在今洛阳市偃师县，位于汉魏洛阳城南郊，遵循"南郊祭天"的传统都城建筑礼制，面积约44000平方米。灵台是汉代专门的天文观测机构，有固定的人员编制，负责天文观测、制定历法等事务。如东汉著名的科学家、文学家张衡曾在公元2世纪两次出任太史令，负责指导灵台工作，在洛阳任职期间设计制造出浑天仪、候风地动仪等先进仪器（图3-8），堪称世界奇迹，编写出《灵宪》《浑天仪图法》等经典天文学著作。东汉洛阳灵台天文学家还在此观测到月亮运行的不均匀性、太阳黑子的形状等状况，并对此做出了科学解释，代表了中国天文科技水平的高超成就。

图 3-8　东汉张衡造候风地动仪复原图

Fig. 3-8　Seismograph (model restored) made by Zhang Heng of the Eastern Han Dynasty

China, which were used specially for making Tang tri-coloured pottery, and also one of the main producing areas of the bluish white porcelain and tri-coloured porcelain in the Tang Dynasty. Ruins of these official kilns were located on both sides of the Huangye River (Dahuangye Village and Xiaohuangye Village) in present Dongzhan Town of Gongyi City where Tang tri-coloured potteries of various kinds were excavated, with the majority of living utensils and funerary wares, including tripods, bowls, basins, kettles, jars, vases, flagons, wine bowls and small handleless wine cups.

Five famous porcelains from official kilns in the Song Dynasty could be mentioned in the same breath—"Ru, Guan, Jun, Ge, and Ding," of which Ru and Jun porcelains were produced in Ruzhou and Yuzhou respectively in Henan Province. Ru porcelain, renowned in the Northern Song Dynasty, ranks first among the five. With its pure and warm glaze, it presents the intrinsic luster of ancient jade, reflecting the delicate and elegant unique aesthetic taste of the traditional Chinese literati and officialdom (Fig. 3-7). Jun porcelain is well-known for the magical colour changing produced by its unique glaze—"one colour in the kiln, thousands of colours out." Jun porcelain is full of artistic beauty for being unique, various, and glisteningly colourful, which has won special favours of the later generations of collectors. There has always been a saying among the folks that "a piece of Jun porcelain is better than piles of fortunes," showing the superb artistic achievements of Jun porcelain.

(5) Astronomical Calendar

The ancient Chinese people attached great importance to astronomical observation and calendar making, which was derived, on one hand, from the absolute reverence for "heaven" by the ruling class since the pre-Qin period, on the other hand, from pressing practical need to distinguish seasons and climates and to predict celestial phenomena to guide agricultural production. As the central political regions in the early dynasties of China as well as the regions of agricultural origin, the middle and lower reaches of the Yellow River were also the earliest birthplaces of astronomical and calendar achievements in China, and made remarkable achievements in the Qin and Han, also in the Sui and Tang dynasties.

Lingtai Observatory Site of the Eastern Han Dynasty in Yanshi County

（6）造纸、印刷术

造纸术、印刷术是古代中国对世界的巨大发明贡献，对人类文明的进步、知识的传播产生了不可估量的推动作用。现代考古成果表明，造纸术最早出现于西汉中期的黄河流域中上游的今陕西、甘肃境内，但纸张质量还很粗糙（图3-9）。至公元2世纪初的东汉和帝时期，掌管宫廷物品制造的宦官尚方令蔡伦，在京师洛阳研制出一种质量上乘、轻便耐用的纸张献给朝廷，此后在全国得以推广，蔡伦因此获封龙亭侯，时人称这种纸为"蔡侯纸"。根据对现代出土东汉纸张的材料学分析，东汉纸张在结构厚度、纤维密度、涂料运用及蒸煮、晾晒工序等方面与现代工艺原则基本一致，具有很高的技术水准。自此以后，纸张的使用在中国得到逐步的推广，替代了传统竹简和丝绸类等笨重、昂贵书写材料，使得文化经典、科技知识保存更为简易方便。公元6—9世纪隋唐时期，雕版印刷术在黄河流域得到逐步的推广普及。造纸术、印刷术由中国渐次传播至东亚的朝鲜、日本等国，并由阿拉伯世界传入欧洲，对世界文明的发展起到了巨大的影响。

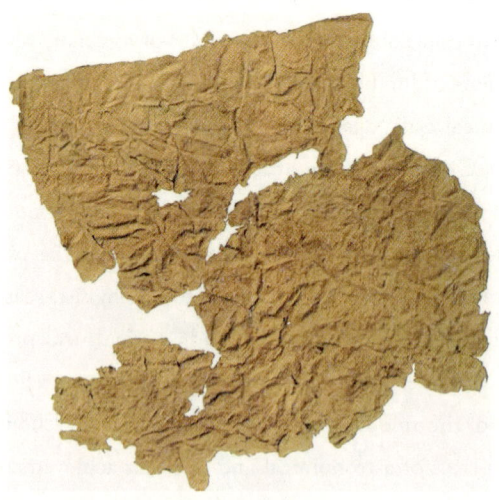

图 3-9　甘肃天水放马滩出土的西汉纸张

Fig. 3-9　Paper of the Western Han Dynasty unearthed at Fangmatan in Tianshui of Gansu Province

of Henan Province is the earliest large astronomical observatory site discovered in China, and the landmark has been showing the outstanding achievements of ancient Chinese astronomy. Located in the present Yanshi County which is in the southern suburb of Luoyang City, it followed the traditional capital building ritual of "worshipping Heaven in the southern suburbs," covering an area of about 44,000 square meters. Lingtai used to be a specialized astronomical observation institution in the Han Dynasty, with fixed staff in charge of astronomical observation, calendar making and other affairs. For example, Zhang Heng, a famous scientist and litterateur in the Eastern Han Dynasty, took the post of Taishiling twice in the 2nd century AD—in charge of its management. During his tenure in Luoyang, he devised the advanced instruments such as Armillary Sphere and Seismograph (Fig. 3-8) which deserved to be wonders of the world, and compiled *Lingxian* (an astronomical book) and *Armillary Sphere* and other classical astronomical works. During the Eastern Han Dynasty, it was right in Lingtai of Luoyang that astronomers also had observation on the inhomogeneity of the moon's movement, the shape of sunspots and so on, and came up with a scientific illustration, which represented the superb achievements of astronomical science and technology.

(6) Papermaking and Printing

Papermaking and printing are the great contributions of ancient China to the world, which have played an immeasurable role in enhancing the progress of human civilization and the spread of knowledge. Modern archaeological findings show that papermaking first appeared in the middle of the Western Han Dynasty in the middle and upper reaches of the Yellow River Basin, which is in today's Shaanxi and Gansu provinces, but the paper quality was crude (Fig. 3-9). During the reign of Emperor Hedi in the Eastern Han Dynasty at the beginning of the 2nd century, Cai Lun, a eunuch, also served as Shangfangling (an official post), took charge of the production of articles for the imperial court, and developed a kind of high-quality, light and durable paper for the imperial court in Luoyang. After that, it became popular all over the country. Cai Lun was thus bestowed the title of "Longting Hou" (Longting Marquis), and this kind of paper was called "Caihou Paper" at that time. Basically, paper made in the Eastern Han Dynasty reached a very high technical level, and was consistent with modern technical

2. 高度发达的城市建设与交通运输网络

城市是人类生产力充分发展的产物，城市的产生是文明进入高度发展阶段的标志之一。中国的城市最早产生于黄河流域，在中原地区分布最为密集。现今考古发现的郑州西山古城遗址、登封王城岗遗址、淮阳平粮台古城遗址，是距今 4000—5000 年前新石器时代仰韶文化、龙山文化的典型城址代表。而偃师二里头城址、郑州商城遗址、安阳殷墟遗址、东周洛阳故城等作为夏、商、周三代的都城遗址蜚声内外。

秦、汉、隋、唐、北宋时期中国的政治、经济中心都位于黄河中下游地区的关中、中原地区。大一统集权王朝能够集中调动全国的人力、物力，投入城市营建和水陆运输网络建设。黄河流域在公元前 2 世纪至公元 12 世纪出现了一批享誉世界的大都市，在建筑面积、人口数量、经济规模上都达到了空前的高度。以都城为核心的交通网络四通八达，延伸至全国各地，水、陆、海运便捷畅通，极大地促进了国内经济的发展和对外贸易的繁荣。

（1）大都市的规划与建设

中国古代对城市尤其是都城的规划理念成熟甚早，《周礼·考工记》有"匠人营国"一章，在都城的建筑布局、朝向、高度、功能区分，以及道路宽度、城门数量等方面都有相应的等级礼制规则。源于《周礼》的都城规划理念基本上被后世封建王朝所遵循，逐步形成了中国古代城市规划以彰显皇权威严为核心，以城郭方正、道路笔直为美，讲究中轴线对称等独特风格。古代黄河流域都市如汉唐长安城、汉魏洛阳城、北宋开封城的城市布局及建筑风格，对中国后世以及周边东亚国家朝鲜、日本、越南产生了深刻的影响。

汉长安城城墙周长达 22 千米，墙基 12—16 米，高 10 米以上，城外有 8 米宽、3 米深的护城河，非常坚固雄伟。每面城墙有 3 道城门，各城门有 3 个门道，道宽 8 米，可供 4 辆马车并行，十分开阔壮观。城内主道纵横，道宽约 45 米，将城市分为宫殿、市场、作坊、民居等不

principles in terms of structure thickness, fiber density, coating application, steaming and drying and other processes. Since then, the paper gained its popularity gradually in China, replacing heavy and expensive writing materials such as traditional bamboo slips and silk, and making preservation of cultural classics and scientific knowledge easier and more convenient. During the Sui and Tang dynasties from the 6th to the 9th century, woodblock printing came to be popular in the Yellow River Basin. Papermaking and printing gradually spread from China to Korea, Japan and other countries in East Asia, and from the Arab countries to Europe, making a massive impact on the development of world civilization.

2. Highly-Developed Urban Construction & Transportation Network

The rise of cities—the product of full development of human productivity, is one of the signs of civilization going into a highly-developed stage. Cities in China first emerged in the Yellow River Basin, most densely distributed in the Central Plains. Xishan Ancient City Site in Zhengzhou, Wangchenggang Site in Dengfeng and Pingliangtai Ancient City Site in Huaiyang are the typical representatives of ancient city sites of the Yangshao Culture and the Longshan Culture during the Neolithic Age 4,000 to 5,000 years ago. Erlitou Site in Yanshi, Shangcheng Ruins in Zhengzhou, Yinxu Ruins in Anyang, and Luoyang Ancient City of the Eastern Zhou Dynasty used to be the capital sites of the Xia, Shang and Zhou dynasties, which gained good reputation both at home and abroad.

From the Qin to Han, and from the Sui to Tang and Northern Song dynasties, China's political and economic centers were all located in Guanzhong or Central Plains of the middle and lower reaches of the Yellow River. A unified and centralized dynasty could achieve concentrated mobilization of manpower and material resources of the whole country to invest in city building and land-water transportation network construction. Therefore, between the 2nd century BC and the 12th century AD, a number of world-renowned metropolises surged in the Yellow River Basin, which reached an unprecedented height in terms of building area, population and economic scale. With the capital as the core, the transportation grid extended in all directions to all parts of the country, making it convenient and smooth by water and land, which greatly enhanced the development of domestic economy and the prosperity of foreign trade.

同区域。城外还有占地广阔的皇家园林上林苑，建筑华丽奢侈，湖泊、花木、珍禽异兽点缀其中，恍若仙境。而唐长安城则更为宏伟，面积达 84 平方千米，为汉长安城的 2.4 倍，是古代世界规模最大的城市（图 3-10）。长安城作为唐朝的政治、经济、文化中心，人口众多，繁华异常，四方域外商旅辐辏，堪称世界之都。

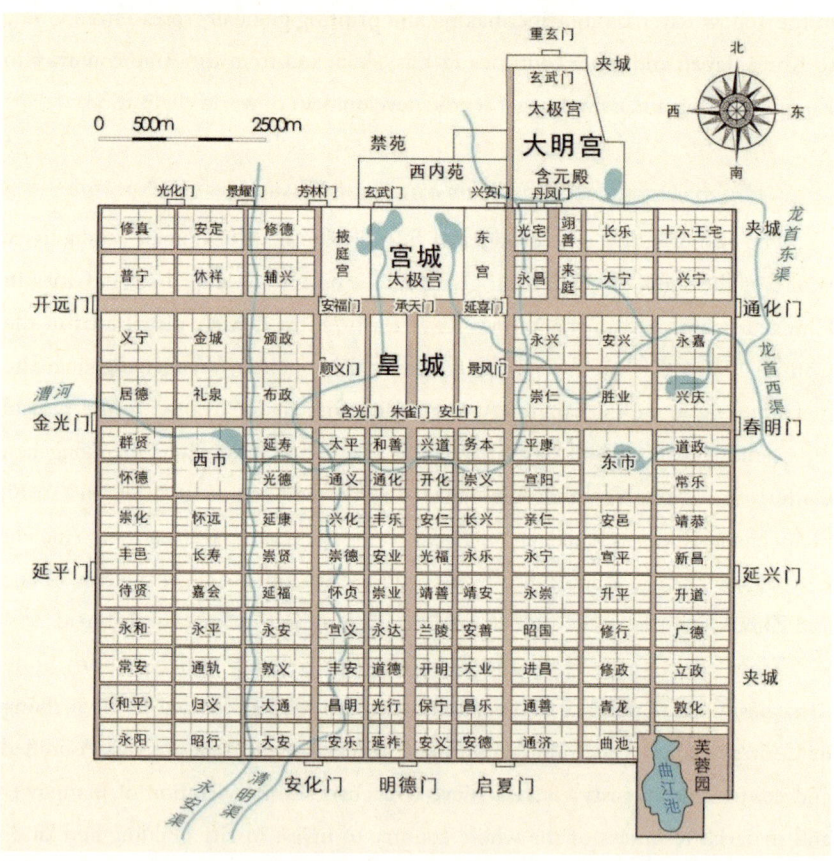

图 3-10　唐长安城布局平面示意图

Fig. 3-10　The layout plan diagram of Chang' an City in the Tang Dynasty

汉魏洛阳城和北宋开封城都位于黄河中下游的河南境内，与汉唐长安城相比，地理位置相对适中，交通便利，商业更加发达。史料记载东

(1) Urban Planning and Construction

In ancient China, the planning of cities, especially capital cities, matured very early. The chapter "Capital City Designing" (documents on various types of work specifications and manufacturing processes in *The Rites of the Zhou Dynasty*) recorded that corresponding rules of hierarchical etiquette were requested for the layout, orientation, height, functional distinction, road width, number of gates and other aspects in the capital city designing. The concept of capital city designing, originated from *The Rites of the Zhou Dynasty*, was basically followed by later feudal dynasties and gradually developed its unique styles—highlighting the imperial majesty as its core, regarding square city walls and straight roads as the beauty, and paying attention to the symmetry of the central axis. The urban layout and architectural style of ancient capital cities along the Yellow River, such as Chang'an in the Han and Tang dynasties, Luoyang in the Han and Wei dynasties, and Kaifeng in the Northern Song Dynasty, exerted a profound influence on later generations of China as well as East Asian countries such as Korea, Japan and Vietnam.

The city walls of Chang'an in the Han Dynasty were 22 kilometers in circumference, with a base of 12 to 16 meters and a height of more than 10 meters, and were very strong and magnificent. Outside the city, there was a moat which was 8 meters wide and 3 meters deep. Each wall had three gates, and each gate had three eight-meter gateways, wide and spectacular, enough for four carriages to pass through at the same time. The city was crisscrossed by the main roads, about 45 meters wide each, dividing the city into different areas of palaces, markets, workshops and folk houses. In the suburb, there were vast royal gardens called Shanglin Imperial Park, gorgeous and luxurious, with lakes, flowers and trees, rare birds and animals dotted inside, like a fairyland. Chang'an in the Tang Dynasty was even more magnificent, with an area of 84 square kilometers, 2.4 times the size of Chang'an in the Han Dynasty, making it the largest city in the ancient world (Fig. 3-10). As the political, economic and cultural center of the Tang Dynasty, Chang'an City, with a large population and extraordinary prosperity, could be called as the capital of the world for business and travel from all directions.

Compared with Chang'an in the Han and Tang dynasties, Luoyang in

汉洛阳境内，商人十倍于农民，各种贩卖四方奢侈品的商人遍布都邑。城市人口规模巨大，仅太学生即一度多达3万人，太学门前曾经乘车日千余辆，引起严重的交通堵塞。而北宋时期由于经济高度发达，开封城更是繁华异常，而且北宋解除了汉唐以来的宵禁制度，打破了隔离生活区和商业区的里坊限制，商业、市井气息更加浓厚，各种娱乐场所通宵达旦营业，热闹非凡。北宋张择端所绘之《清明上河图》，活灵活现地呈现了北宋开封城的发达与繁荣，成为流传至今的不朽巨作。

（2）水陆交通网络的完善

秦汉、隋唐等封建王朝十分重视官方驿道的建设，往往不定期征调大量的民夫对道路进行修筑及维护，沿途还设立驿站负责过往官员、商旅的接待事宜，并设置专门的巡查警戒机构确保驿道行途的安全。在此时期，历代王朝以黄河流域为中心，逐步构建出完善、紧密的水陆交通网络，实现了政令传达的畅通以及物资运输、贸易往来的便捷迅速，形成了一批区域政治、商业中心。

秦始皇统一六国之后，立即以咸阳为中心修筑延伸至全国的驰道，道宽50步，道旁隔3丈植松树一株为障。至两汉时期，随着全国道路网络的完善和河西走廊通道的开辟，以长安和洛阳为起点，逐步形成了沟通中西、举世闻名的丝绸之路。此外值得注意的是，由于成本低、效率高、更加安全的特点，水路运输一直备受中国历代王朝的青睐，水运交通网络逐渐成为国家经济命脉所系，堪称古代世界的"高速公路"。如举世闻名的隋唐大运河，以中原地区的洛阳为中心，在历代旧运河的基础上，沟通海河、黄河、淮河、长江水系，形成了贯通南北、东西的交通大动脉，对全国经济的发展起到了巨大的推动作用，对后世中国政治、经济格局的变迁也产生了重大的影响（图3-11）。此后北宋定都开封，即与开封周边水系密布、运河网络完善，处于沟通黄河水系和东南淮河、长江水系的中心地位有莫大的关系。

the Han and Wei dynasties and Kaifeng in the Northern Song Dynasty were both located in Henan Province, which was in the middle and lower reaches of the Yellow River. Their geographical locations were relatively moderate with convenient transportation and more developed commerce. Historical records showed that businessmen in Luoyang during the Eastern Han Dynasty outnumbered farmers ten to one and merchants selling luxury goods could be seen everywhere. The urban population was enormous, in which students of the Imperial College once reached more than 30,000 and vehicles for them were more than 1,000 daily, which ever caused serious traffic jams. While in the Northern Song Dynasty, due to the highly-developed economy, Kaifeng was even more prosperous. Moreover, the curfew system of the Han and Tang dynasties was then broken, and the lane restriction that separated the living areas from the commercial ones was cancelled. The atmosphere of commerce and market became stronger, and all kinds of entertainment places opened all night and were very lively. *Riverside Scene on the Pure Brightness Festival* painted by Zhang Zeduan in the Northern Song Dynasty depicts the bustling scene of flourishment and prosperity in Kaifeng at that time, which is an immortal masterpiece handed down to today.

(2) Improvement of Land-Water Transportation Network

Feudal dynasties such as the Qin, Han, Sui and Tang dynasties attached great importance to the construction of official post roads, and often recruited a large number of civilian workers to build and maintain the roads from time to time. Along the way, post stations were established to take charge of the receptions for officials and trade caravans passing by, and special warning patrol agencies were set up to guard the safety. During this period, many a dynasty took the Yellow River Basin as the center and gradually built perfect and close land-water transportation networks. The transmission of government decrees became smooth, and materials transportation and trade grew rapid and convenient, therefore, a number of regional political and commercial centers came into being.

Emperor Shihuang (the First Emperor of the Qin Dynasty) immediately ordered to build Chidao (mail roads) extending to the whole territory with Xianyang as the center after he unified the six kingdoms. The road was 50 bu (unit of length, one bu is about 0.4-0.6 meters) wide and a pine tree was planted

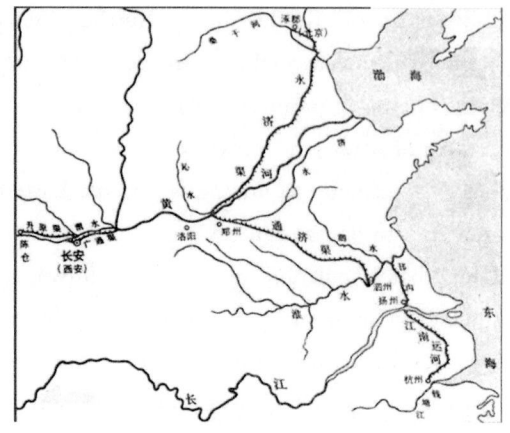

图 3–11　隋唐运河示意图

史念海：《中国的运河》，陕西人民出版社，1988 年

Fig. 3–11　The sketch map of the Sui–Tang Grand Canal

Shi Nianhai: *The Canals in China*, Shaanxi People's Press, 1988

3. 世界领先的政治体制创造和国家政权建设

早期世界重大文明都诞生于大河流域，如古埃及、古巴比伦、古印度文明分别产生于尼罗河、幼发拉底河、恒河流域，而古中国文明则发源于黄河流域，故黄河被称为中国的母亲河。以上四大文明古国之中，只有以黄河文化为根源的中华文明一直绵延不绝，至今昌盛。除了中华文明所处得天独厚的地理环境因素之外，还与黄河文化的早熟特质和现实理性特点有很大的关系。自西周以来的早期中华文明，逐步把神权与宗教隔离出现实政权，发展出一套以人为本、推崇仁义道德、讲究宗族礼法、重视行政制度建设的国家治理体系，通过不断的调整和完善，形成了鲜明的东亚黄河文明特色。

（1）缜密完备的官僚选用、考核、监察体制

反映西周制度的《周礼》一书，相传为周初的周公旦所作。其书以天官冢宰、地官司徒、春官宗伯、夏官司马、秋官司寇、冬官百工为"六官"，各辖所属吏员，负责国家民政、宗族、法律及营造等各类事务，已经呈现出专门化、细致化的官僚政治倾向（图 3–12）。至秦始皇统

every 3 zhang (unit of length, one zhang is about 3.33 meters) apart as a barrier. During the Han Dynasty, with the improvement of the national road network and the opening of the Hexi Corridor, starting from Chang'an and Luoyang, the world-famous Silk Road connecting China and the West gradually took shape. It is also worth noting that due to the advantages of low cost, high efficiency and safety, water transportation was favored by successive dynasties in China. This network gradually became the lifeline of the national economy and was regarded as the "highway" of the ancient world. Take the world-renowned Sui-Tang Grand Canal as an example, on the previous basis, it made a connection with the Haihe River, the Yellow River, the Huaihe River and the Yangtze River, with Luoyang in the Central Plains as its center. As the major traffic artery running through from north to south, and east to west, the Sui-Tang Grand Canal played a tremendous role in promoting the development of national economy, with a significant impact on reshaping the political and economic map of China in later generations (Fig. 3-11). Since then, Kaifeng was founded as the capital of the Northern Song Dynasty, which was undoubtedly related to the dense surrounding water systems and perfect canal network, as well as the central position of linking the Yellow River system with the Huaihe River and the Yangtze River system in the southeast.

3. Creation of the World-Leading Political System and Construction of State Power

Major civilizations in the early stage of the world were all born in large river basins, such as ancient Egypt, ancient Babylon and ancient India, which were born in the Nile, Euphrates and Ganges respectively, while the ancient Chinese civilization originated in the Yellow River Basin. Therefore, the Yellow River has always been regarded as the Mother River of China. Amidst the above four ancient civilizations, only the Chinese civilization rooted in the Yellow River culture remains flourishing without cease. In addition to advantaged geographical environment in which Chinese civilization is located, it also has a strong connection with the precocious and realistic characteristics of the Yellow River culture. The early Chinese civilization since the Western Zhou Dynasty gradually segregated theocracy and religion from the actual political power and developed

一中国后,废分封而设郡县,中央集权的官僚政治得以确立,依靠庞大但各有专责的官僚队伍,实现对全国人口、资源的高效控制和整合。经过秦代官僚政治的强力整合,以黄河中下游地区为整体依托的中国稳定政治、文化中心基本形成。

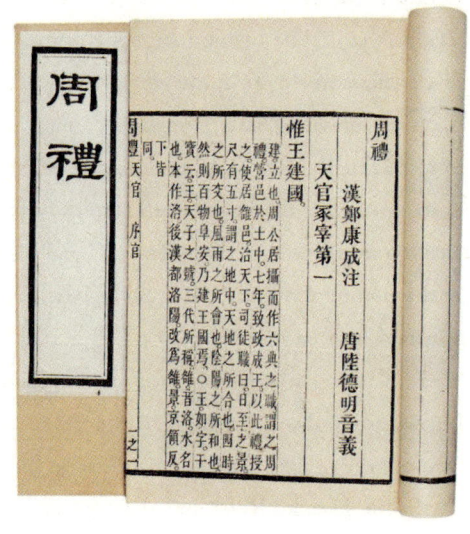

图 3-12 《周礼》
Fig. 3-12 The Rites of the Zhou Dynasty

　　秦代官僚行政制度的流动选拔性、功绩考核制、权力制约原则,基本为后世所遵循。在汉代及魏晋还逐步形成品评德才以推荐官员的察举制、九品中正制,至隋唐时期发展为以考试选官的科举制度,成为现代文官选拔制度雏形。秦汉时期还形成常规化的官员考核制度,以年度为单位,地方官员"上计"土地开垦面积、赋税收入、人口增长情况,上级主管部门依据下属表现考评为上、中、下等不同等级,据此对官员进行黜陟。秦汉时期中央设置御史大夫等官员专职监察百官;汉代设十三道监察御史分巡地方,纠举、弹劾不法官员;唐代依据全国地理形势,分全国为十道(后增至十五道)监察区域。汉、唐时期,国家监察机构权力呈现逐渐增强趋势,甚至架空地方郡县行政权力,从不定期、不定

a set of national governance system—people-oriented, advocating benevolence, righteousness and virtues, paying attention to clan rites and legislations, and attaching great importance to administration construction, which took the shape of distinctive features of the Yellow River civilization in East Asia with constant adjustment and improvement.

(1) Rigorous and Complete System of Selection, Assessment and Supervision for Bureaucrats

It is said that *The Rites of the Zhou Dynasty*—a book reflecting the system of the Western Zhou, was written by Duke of Zhou who named Dan at the early Zhou Dynasty. In the book, "Six Officials" refer to officials of Heaven Zhongzai (assisting the emperor in civil administration), Earth Situ (assisting the emperor in land affairs), Spring Zongbo (assisting the emperor in royal house affairs), Summer Sima (assisting the emperor in military affairs), Autumn Sikou (assisting the emperor in justice), and Winter Baigong (assisting the emperor in constructions). They should rule over their subordinates and take charge of the civil affairs, clans, laws, constructions and other kinds of affairs, presenting a specialized and detailed bureaucratic political tendency (Fig. 3-12). After the Qin's unification, with the abolition of enfeoffment system and the founding of prefecture and county system, a centralized bureaucracy was set up, relying on a large but dedicated team of bureaucrats to achieve efficient control and integration of the country's population and resources. After the powerful integration of the bureaucracy in the Qin Dynasty, a stable political and cultural center based on the middle and lower reaches of the Yellow River practically took shape in China.

Later generations generally followed the Qin's principles of mobile selection, merit examination and power restriction in the bureaucratic administrative system. The Recommendation System in the Han Dynasty and Nine-Grade-Officials System in the Wei and Jin dynasties were gradually formed to recommend officials judging by their morals and virtues. In the Sui and Tang dynasties, the Imperial Examination System was developed to select officials by examination, which became the prototype of modern civil servant selection system. In the Qin and Han dynasties, a regular official assessment system was also established for the superior to assess the performance of their subordinates into different levels— upper, middle and lower to promote or depose accordingly based on

员的巡视机构成为新一级的实体权力机构。

（2）层级分明的中央及地方行政制度

秦代在中央设立"三公九卿"，以丞相、太尉、御史大夫为"三公"分领全国民政、军事、监察事务，辅佐皇帝行使最高权力，以奉常、郎中令、卫尉、廷尉、少府等"九卿"负责皇室内廷、祭祀、司法、税收等具体事务。而在南至南海、北达辽东的广袤国土设置郡县，以太守、县令统领地方行政事务，各具僚佐以辅助治理。各级中央、地方官僚的任命、调动都源自皇帝的最高指令，无法世袭。这样，以皇权为核心的高度中央集权政体正式得到确立，强大的大一统国家具备了前代无法比拟的动员力量，对中国幅员辽阔疆域的形成和对地方的有效治理奠定了基础。汉代在继承秦代行政体制的基础上，在地方行政上由原来的郡、县二级制演化为州、郡、县三级制。州最高长官为刺史，原为中央派出巡视不同地理区域的监察官员，后演化为统属郡县的行政官员。行政层级的增多，是国家行政分工越来越具体、纤细化的现实需要，有利于中央对地方的有效控制。

唐代中央行政制度发展为"三省六部制"，以中书、尚书、门下三省长官为宰辅决策，以尚书省下辖之"吏、礼、兵、户、刑、工"六部为具体事务执行机构（图3–13）。三省系统需要相互配合但又互相制约，在决策、审核、执行层面各有专责，在职能层面并无重叠，有利于减少分歧内耗，实现决策合理化和执行高效化；把混淆皇帝私家事务和国家事务职责的"九卿"，剥离出国家行政体系，代之以权责分明、分工细致的"六部"，对皇帝"家天下"体制下的内廷职能进行约束，对行政效率的提高起到了积极的作用。相较于秦汉的"三公九卿制"，唐代"三省六部制"更加成熟合理，具有明显的现代行政色彩，是中国古代政治文明成果的典型代表。

their "annual report" of land reclamation area, tax revenue and population growth. During the Qin and Han dynasties, the central government set posts such as the imperial censor to supervise all officials. In the Han Dynasty, there were 13 posts for supervising censors to patrol the localities to rectify and impeach the illegal officials. Based on the geographical situation, the whole Tang kingdom was divided into ten (later increased to fifteen) supervisory regions. During the Han and Tang dynasties, the power of national supervisory offices strengthened gradually, the administrative power of local prefectures and counties was even eliminated, and the patrol offices which patrolled irregularly with irregular personnel became a new grade of entity authority.

(2) Central and Local Administrative Systems with Clear Hierarchies

The system of "Three Councilors and Nine Ministers" was set up as the leadership of the Qin Dynasty. "Three Councilors"—Chengxiang (prime minister), Taiwei (chief commander) and Yushidafu (imperial censor) took charge of the civil affairs, military affairs and supervision of the country, assisting the emperor in his supreme power. "Nine Ministers" like Fengchang (for etiquettes of royal ancestral temples), Langzhongling (for royal palace guards), Weiwei (for royal palace gate guards), Tingwei (for justice and punishment), and Shaofu (for taxation and the emperor's living supplies) performed their duties in specific affairs of the imperial court, sacrificial rites, judicial affairs and taxation. While in the vast territory stretching from the South China Sea in the south to Liaodong in the north, prefects and county magistrates were in charge of local administration, each with their own subordinate staff to assist in governance. The appointments and transfers of central and local bureaucrats at all levels were at the command of the supreme instructions of the emperor and could not be hereditary. By doing so, the highly-centralized government with the imperial power as the core was formally established, and the powerful unified country had the mobilization power that the previous generation could not match, which laid the foundation for the formation of China's vast territory and effective governance of local areas. On the basis of inheriting the Qin's system, the Han's local administration evolved from the original two-level system of prefecture and county to the three-level system—state, prefecture and county. The state head was Cishi, who was originally a supervisory official dispatched from the central government to tour and inspect

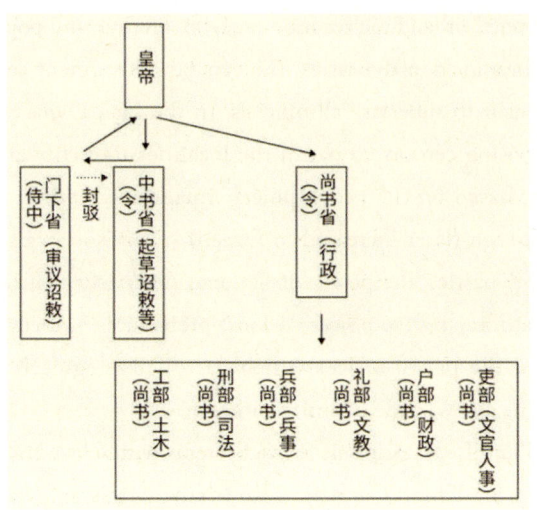

图3-13 唐代"三省六部制"示意图
Fig. 3-13 The diagram of "Three Ministries and Six Departments" in the Tang Dynasty

(3) 礼法合一、法治与德治并重的法制体系

中国向来以礼仪之邦著称。礼起源于原始社会以来的社会习惯和宗族秩序,在中国商、周时代的黄河中下游地区即形成了一套完整而成熟的社会礼仪规范。而法的兴起则在春秋战国时期,传统的西周宗法礼仪制度逐渐解体,出现礼崩乐坏的混乱局面,社会上逐渐兴起一股强调刑罚、讲究事功主义以维持秩序、富国强兵的社会思潮,史称"法家"。以商鞅主导的一系列变法措施最为成功,最终实现了中国第一个集权制大一统帝国——秦国的诞生。但秦国以法家为主导的治国思想过于强调刑罚威权,在执行层面过于刚性严酷,导致了秦朝二世而亡。继之而起的汉王朝吸取教训,确立以礼治和德治为核心的儒家思想为国家意识形态主流,但在行政执行层面亦结合秦代法治思想,形成"霸王道杂之"——德治和法治相结合的治国思想,即以伦理教化为指导、以实际案例总结为依托的法律体系构建。其原则基本为后世封建王朝所遵循,逐步形成

different areas, and later evolved into an administrative official. The increase of administrative levels met the practical need of national administrative division which became more and more specific and detailed, and was conducive to effective control of the central government over local areas.

In the Tang Dynasty, the central government administration developed into "Three Ministries and Six Departments," with the governors of the "Three Ministries" (Zhongshu, Shangshu and Menxia) as subsidiary policy-making officials, and the "Six Departments"—Li (official), Li (ritual), Bing (military), Hu (household), Xing (justice), and Gong (labor) as executive agencies of specific affairs under the jurisdiction of Shangshu (Fig. 3-13). The "Three Ministries" system needed both cooperation and restriction with each other. Each ministry had special duties in policy-making, verification and implementation, and there was no overlap in functions, which was conducive to reducing internal frictions and realizing rationalization of policy-decision and high efficiency of implementation. The "Nine Ministers" system that used to confuse the emperor's private affairs with those of the kingdom was stripped out of the national administration yet replaced with "Six Departments" which had distinct powers and obligations with detailed divisions. It restrained the functions of the imperial court under the emperor's "Family Rule" system and played a positive role in improving administrative efficiency. Compared with the Qin and Han dynasties, the Tang's "Three Ministries and Six Departments" system was more mature and rational, with obvious modern administrative color, and was a typical model of the achievements of ancient Chinese political civilization.

(3) Legal System of Integration of Propriety and Legislation with Equal Stress on Law & Virtue

China has always been famous for its rites. The rites originated from social customs and clan orders since the primitive society, and developed into a set of complete and mature social etiquette norms in the middle and lower reaches of the Yellow River in the Shang and Zhou dynasties. During the Spring and Autumn Period and the Warring States Period, the Legislation emerged when the traditional Western Zhou patriarchal clan and etiquette system gradually disintegrated, resulting in the chaotic situation of propriety collapse. Therefore, a social trend of thought arose, which emphasized punishment, advocated

礼法合一的法制思想，至唐代发展为律令完备、高度成熟的法律制度（图3-14），其影响波及整个东亚大陆。

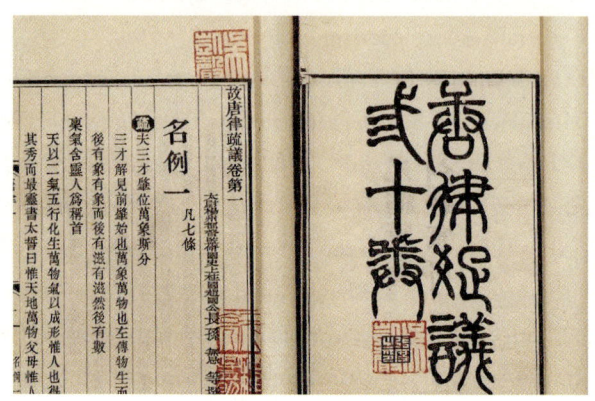

图3-14 中国古代经典律令《唐律疏议》

Fig. 3-14 Classical laws and regulations in ancient China—*Comments on the Laws of the Tang Dynasty*

（4）刚柔并济、注重民生的治国思想

西周时代一直被中国传统文化阶层认为是古典政治的模范时代，周代的治国思想中已经体现出较为强烈的关注民生的现实理性色彩。至春秋时期，各种政治思想竞相涌现，诸子百家争鸣登场，堪称中国文化思想奠基的"轴心时代"。儒家、法家、墨家、道家、纵横家等各种政治流派，经过长时期的融合，最终在西汉形成了以儒家为主导，借鉴吸收法家、道家思想的中国传统治国思想。既有自强不息、开创进取的原始儒家、法家刚性特点，又兼具清静无为、与民休息，强调"治大国若烹小鲜"的早期道家思想柔性特质。把施行仁政、推崇道义作为国家政权合法性的首要条件，并萌生出"民贵君轻"的民本主义思想（图3-15）。中国早期王朝这些刚柔相济、强调民生的现实理性主义治国思想形成，在约束君权、禁止暴虐苛政、维护社会长治久安等方面起到了十分重要的基础作用。而这些思想的产生、发展和实践的核心区域，都位于黄河中下游区域这一政治中心地带。

utilitarianism to maintain order, and prospered the country and strengthened the army, known as "Legalism" in history. The first centralized and unified kingdom—Qin should be attributed to the series of most successful reforms led by Shang Yang. However, the Legalism went too far in authoritarian punishment and was too rigid and harsh in execution, which led to quick downfall of the Qin in its second generation. Very soon it came to the Han that learned the Qin's lessons and established Confucianism with the governance by propriety & by virtue as the mainstream of national ideology. Meanwhile, as for its administrative execution, the Han took Legalism of the Qin into consideration, developing "a hybrid governance by rulers" —both virtues and legislation, namely, the construction of a legal system guided by ethical education and based on the summary of practical cases. In general, its principles were followed by later feudal dynasties, gradually comprising the legal system of integration of propriety and legislation, and developing into a well-regulated and highly-mature legal system in the Tang Dynasty (Fig. 3-14), whose impact spread to the entire East Asian Continent.

(4) Administrative Theory of Focusing on People's Livelihood and Converging of Force and Mercy

The Western Zhou Dynasty has always been regarded as the model era of classical politics by the traditional Chinese intellectuals. The Zhou's administration

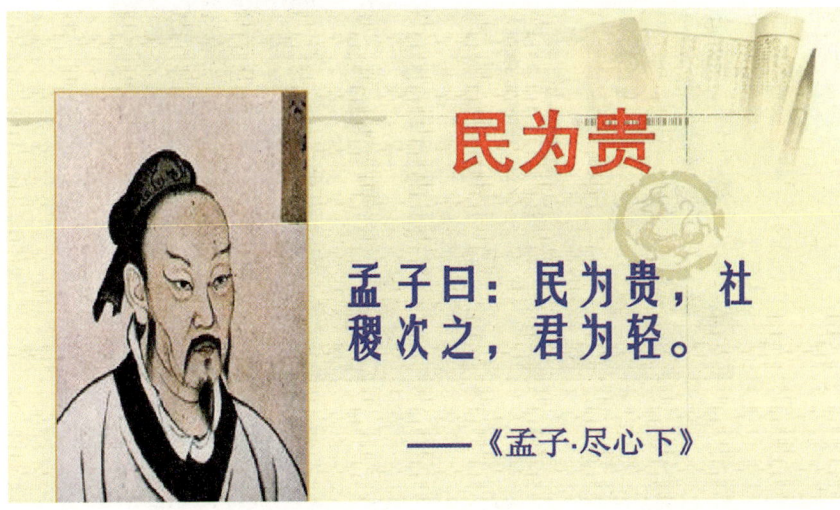

图 3-15 孟子"民为贵"思想

Fig. 3-15 "The people weigh most while a monarch least" by Mencius

4. 灿烂丰富的文化典籍形成和引领东亚的思想流派涌现

从先秦至唐宋时期，随着黄河流域生产力的不断提高和区域交流的持续增强，以黄河流域中下游地区为核心的稳定政治、文化中心逐渐定型，涌现出光辉灿烂的精神文明成果。以儒家文化为代表的中华文化不断与时俱进、开拓创新，向四周辐射传播，逐渐形成了中国乃至东亚地区统一稳固的文化认同和审美情趣。

（1）儒家文化

儒家文化是中华传统文化的中流砥柱，是2000余年的中国封建时代国家意识形态的主流核心。儒家思想产生、形成于黄河中下游的周代文化核心区域。儒家思想起源于西周时期的礼乐文化，由孔子及其弟子孟子、荀子等在春秋时期重新阐释，最终形成一个对中国影响深远的政治思想、哲学、文化体系，后世又称"孔孟之道"（图3-16）。儒家思想讲究仁义、礼法、信用、宽恕，重视友爱、和睦、孝顺的伦理道德，以实现"天下为公、选贤与能、讲信修睦、老有所养"的理想社会状态——"大同社会"为终极目标。儒家文化在两汉、魏晋、隋唐、北宋时期不

图 3-16 儒家经典：四书五经

Fig. 3-16 Confucian classics: the Four Books and the Five Classics

The Four Books (*The Great Learning*, *The Doctrine of the Mean*, *The Analects of Confucius*, and *The Works of Mencius*) and the Five Classics (*The Book of Songs*, *The Book of History*, *The Book of Changes*, *The Book of Rites* and *The Spring and Autumn Annals*)

has reflected a strong concern for people's livelihood with realistic and rational colour. In the Spring and Autumn Period, different political thoughts emerged one after another and various schools came on stage, which could be acclaimed "Axis Age" that laid the foundation of Chinese cultural thought. After a long period of integration, various political schools, such as Confucianism, Legalism, Mohism, Taoism, and Political Strategists, eventually constituted the traditional Chinese statecraft in the Western Han Dynasty in which Confucianism took the lead, borrowing and absorbing Legalism and Taoism. It had not only "force" in pioneering for creation and striving for self-improvement of the original Confucianism and rigid Legalism, but also "mercy" in flexibilities of early Taoism, which emphasized "governing a big country is like cooking a small fish." The traditional Chinese statecraft took humanity and morality as the priority of the legitimacy of state power, showing people-oriented thought of "the people weigh most while a monarch least (Fig. 3-15)." In the early Chinese dynasties, realist and rationalist governance ideas that had both "force" and "mercy" and emphasized people's livelihood came into being, which served as a very important foundation in restraining monarchy, prohibiting tyranny and maintaining social stability. Moreover, the emergence, development and practice of these ideas all centered on the key political zone of the middle and lower reaches of the Yellow River.

4. Formation of Splendid Cultural Classics and Surge of Schools of Thought that Took the Lead in East Asia

From pre-Qin period to the Tang and Song dynasties, with continuous flourishment of productivity in the Yellow River Basin and sustainable enhancement of regional exchanges, the stable political and cultural center, with the middle and lower reaches of the Yellow River as the core, gradually took shape, and splendid achievements of spiritual civilization emerged. The Chinese culture represented by Confucian culture kept pace with the times, advancing with innovation and spreading out in all directions, and gradually formed a unified and stable cultural identity and aesthetics of China and even East Asia.

(1) Confucian Culture

Confucian culture is the mainstay of traditional Chinese culture and the mainstream core of national ideology during the feudal period of more than two

断发展，吸收不同思想的优点，内涵亦不断丰富，形成了蔚为壮观的文化典籍和风格鲜明的思想流派，如兴盛于关中和中原地区的两汉经学、魏晋玄学、宋代理学等学说。经过历代儒家学者的注疏阐释，借鉴道家、佛教思想的精髓之处，儒家文化不断焕发出新的生机活力，最终造就了以儒家文化为主体、多元包容的中华文化。

（2）史学与史书

中国具有悠久而出色的史学传统，从先秦至两汉、唐、宋时期，从黄河流域孕育出的史学得到长足的发展，产生了灿若群星的经典史书著作。

体例逐渐完备：有编年体、国别体、纪传体、纪事本末体等。如孔子所编《春秋》，是中国现存第一部编年体史书，言简意赅而藏褒贬大义，被后世敬称为"春秋笔法""微言大义"；战国时期产生的《国语》《战国策》等国别体史书，文辞纵横、生动优美，成为中国古代外交辞令的渊薮；西汉司马迁所撰《史记》（图3-17），开创私人编修纪传体史书先河，具有很高的史学和文学价值，有"史家之绝唱，无韵之离骚"之誉，其后的《汉书》、《后汉书》、《三国志》、"唐修八史"等史书，形成了绵延不绝的官修正史传统。

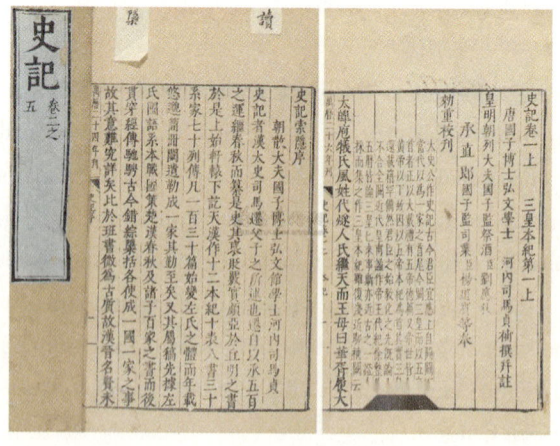

图 3-17 司马迁《史记》

Fig.3-17 *The Great Historical Records* by Sima Qian

thousand years. Confucianism was born and developed in the cultural center of the Zhou Dynasty in the middle and lower reaches of the Yellow River. Confucianism originated from the rites and music culture of the Western Zhou Dynasty, which was reinterpreted by Confucius and his disciples Mencius and Xuncius in the Spring and Autumn Period, and finally developed into a system of political thought, philosophy and culture with far-reaching influence on China, later known as "the Doctrine of Confucius and Mencius" (Fig. 3-16). Confucianism stresses humanity, propriety, faith and forgiveness, attaching great importance to ethics of love, harmony and filial piety. It aims to reach the ultimate goal of "the Great Harmony Society," the ideal social state of "the whole world as one community, selecting the capable and virtuous, practicing faith and good will, and supporting the elderly." Confucian culture continued to develop in the Han, Wei, Jin, Sui, Tang and Northern Song dynasties, soaking nutrients of different thoughts and enriching its connotation, and eventually formed spectacular cultural classics and distinctive schools such as the Study of Confucian Classics of Eastern Han and Western Han dynasties, Metaphysics of the Wei and Jin dynasties, Neo-Confucianism of the Song Dynasty etc., which flourished in Guanzhong and the Central Plains of China. Through the annotation and explanation of Confucian scholars and the reference to the essence of Taoist and Buddhist thoughts, Confucian culture had imbued with new vitality and finally created the inclusive Chinese culture with Confucian culture as the main body.

(2) Historiography and History Books

China has a long and outstanding tradition of historiography. From the pre-Qin period to the Han, Tang and Song dynasties, historiography made considerable progress in the Yellow River Basin and produced outstanding classical history books.

Gradually Complete Styles: There are chronological style, national style, biographical style, and event-based narrative style. For example, *Chunqiu* (*The Spring and Autumn Annals*), compiled by Confucius, is the first chronological history book in China in existence, which is comprehensive and concise, implying praise or criticism. It has been known as "Chunqiu Style" (a style of writing in which sublime words have deep meaning) and "subtle interpretation of great meaning." In the Warring States Period, *Guoyu* (*The Discourse of the States*)

内容愈加丰富：从宫廷编纂的帝王起居注、实录，到地方修撰的方志、图经、风俗传，再到私人传记、野史杂闻等，无所不备；如唐代即形成完整的帝王起居注、日历、时政记等史官记录制度，并要求史官秉笔直书，"不掩恶，不虚美"；汉代即出现《华阳国志》《南阳风俗传》等地方史志作品，至唐代修纂《元和郡县图志》，开创官修全国方志之始。

理论趋于成熟：史学家的视野逐渐开阔，产生了一批史学理论和批评专著。如唐代刘知几所撰《史通》，为中国第一部系统的史学理论著作，对历代史学源流、编纂体例、修史原则等进行了精辟的总结。此外，唐代还出现了《通典》《唐会要》等史书，开创专门对历代典章制度汇纂、批评的政书类史学专著先河。

（3）诗词歌赋

古代中国素以文献之邦著称，历代优秀的文学艺术作品层出不穷，宛若滔滔黄河，澎湃激扬，百川汇流，形成蔚为大观的中华民族独特情感表达方式，展现出鲜明的黄河流域农耕文化特色，给世界留下了丰富多彩的文学宝藏遗产。其中诗、词、歌、赋等文学作品的艺术表现最为灿烂夺目，堪称瑰宝。

春秋中叶出现的中国第一部诗歌总集《诗经》，搜集了西周、东周时期约500年间的诗歌300余篇，诗歌主题从爱情、婚姻、宴会，到战争、政治、农作、动植物等，包罗万象，生动地呈现了周代黄河流域的社会风貌。《诗经》具有强烈浓厚的艺术感染力，展现了中国先民淳朴热烈的情感倾诉方式，被孔子盛赞为："《诗》三百，一言以蔽之，曰：思无邪！"《诗经》后来成为儒家经典"五经"之一，对中国诗歌文学创作产生了重大的影响。

汉代文学以乐府诗和汉赋著称。著名的汉乐府《孔雀东南飞》十分典型地体现了乐府诗采自民间、关注现实题材的现实主义传统；汉赋则讲究辞藻华丽、引用广博、夸张排比，如东汉张衡的《二京赋》，贴切传神地表达出汉代黄河流域繁荣奢侈的城市生活风貌，展现出汉代重视

and *Zhanguoce* (*Strategies of the Warring States*) and other history books whose writing was vivid and graceful with a country as a unit, became the collection of the best ancient Chinese diplomatic parlance. *Shiji* (*The Great Historical Records*) (Fig. 3-17), written by Sima Qian in the Western Han Dynasty, pioneered a private biographical compiling with high historical and literary value, and was reputed as "the first and last great work by historians, the sorrow of separation without rhymes." Later history books such as *Hanshu* (*History of the Han Dynasty*), *Houhanshu* (*History of the Later Han Dynasty*), *Sanguozhi* (*The History of the Three Kingdoms*), and "Eight History Books Compiled in the Tang Dynasty," formed a stretching tradition of official compilation of history books.

More Diverse Contents: From royal edition of notes and records on emperors' daily lives, to local compilation of chorography, books with illustrations and maps, and records of customs, to personal biographies, unofficial histories and so on, the contents were all-inclusive. For example, in the Tang Dynasty, a complete system of records for historians was set for the notes on emperors' daily lives, calendars and current political affairs. Meanwhile historians were required to write straight down the truth, "neither hide evil, nor conceal beauty." In the Han Dynasty, *Records of Huayang*, *Records of Nanyang Customs* and other local historical works came into being. Till the Tang Dynasty, *Map of Yuanhe County* was revised, which marked the beginning of official compilation of local chronicles throughout the country.

Gradually Mature Theory: Historians got to broaden their horizons and came up with a number of historical theories and critical monographs. Such as *Shitong*, written by Liu Zhiji of the Tang Dynasty—the first systematic work of historical theories in China, gave an insightful summary of the origin of historical studies, styles and principles of history compilation. In addition, *Tongdian* and *Tanghuiyao* and other history books in the Tang Dynasty pioneered the treatise on political history that specialized in summarizing and criticizing the laws and institutional systems of the past dynasties.

(3) Chinese Traditional Literature (Poetry, Ci Poetry, Ode, Fu)

Ancient China was renowned as a land of literature, whose outstanding literary and artistic works in successive dynasties emerged one after another, just

现世物质享受的社会风尚,也体现出乐观激扬的中华文化青年期审美取向。经过魏晋南北朝的反思、积淀与创新,中国诗歌在唐代进入黄金时期,呈现出万紫千红、绚丽夺目的艺术色彩,各种流派争奇斗艳,风格各异,涌现出群星闪耀的诗人群体。"诗圣"杜甫(图 3-18)、"诗仙"李白等杰出诗人若高山巍峨,在整个东亚汉文化圈产生了不可磨灭的巨大影响。继唐诗之后,源自于民间市井乐曲的"词"在宋代大放异彩。与"诗以言志"的宏大叙事主题不同,词更注重个人情感的表达,更加细腻婉转、活泼自由,与宋代高度发展的市井世俗社会密切相关,是中国文学发展的另一个高峰。唐诗、宋词并列成为中国文学艺术代表性符号,是唐宋时期黄河文化繁荣发展的典型象征,成为后世中华儿女共同的文化寄托和精神家园。

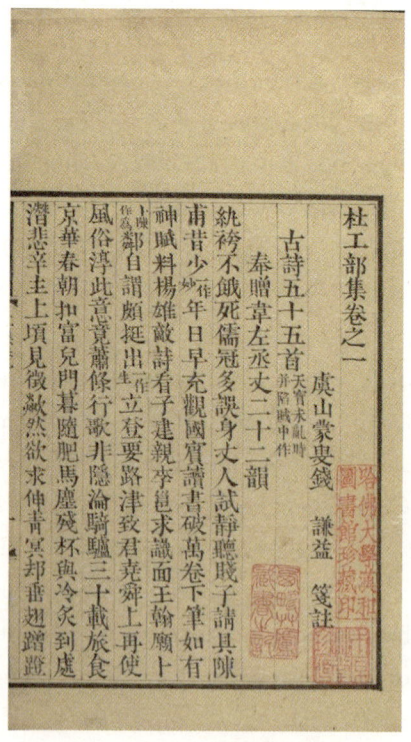

图 3-18 唐代大诗人杜甫诗集

Fig. 3-18 A volume of poems of the great poet Du Fu in the Tang Dynasty

like the running Yellow River surging on. The confluence of all rivers and streams, presenting a splendid sight to show the unique expression of emotion of Chinese nation, displayed the distinct characteristics of farming culture in the Yellow River Basin, and left the world a rich and colorful literary heritage. Among them, Poetry, Ci Poetry, Ode, Fu (Prose Poetry) and other literary works of artistic expression were the most dazzling, which could be boasted as treasures.

The Book of Songs was the first collection of Chinese poetry in the middle of the Spring and Autumn Period, collecting more than 300 poems from the Western and Eastern Zhou dynasties over 500 years. The themes were all-inclusive, covering a wide range from love, marriage, banquets, to wars, politics, farming, plants and animals, vividly presenting the social features of the Yellow River Basin in the Zhou Dynasty. *The Book of Songs* had a strong artistic appeal, showing the simple and passionate way of emotional outpouring of Chinese ancestors. Confucius highly praised it as "All three hundred poems of *The Book of Songs* could be summed up as—simple and true!" Later it became one of the Confucian classics— "the Five Classics," which exerted a great influence on the creation of Chinese poetry and literature.

The literature in the Han Dynasty was famous for Yuefu Poetry (poetry collected in the Music Bureau) and Han Fu (Prose Poetry). The famous *Peacock Flying Southeast* was a typical embodiment of realistic tradition of Yuefu poems which were drawn from the folks and focused on realistic themes. Han Fu emphasized flowery rhetoric, extensive citation, exaggeration and parallelism. *Ode to Two Capitals* by Zhang Heng of the Eastern Han Dynasty vividly expressed the prosperous and luxurious urban lifestyle of the Yellow River Basin, demonstrated social fashion of valuing secular material enjoyment, and reflected optimistic and encouraging aesthetic orientation of Chinese culture in its youth. After reflection, accumulation and innovation in the Wei, Jin and Southern and Northern dynasties, Chinese poetry entered the golden age in the Tang Dynasty, presenting a riot of colors and dazzling artistic colors. Various schools of poetry contended with each other with different styles, and a group of star-lit poets emerged. "Poet Sage" Du Fu (Fig. 3-18) and "Poet Immortal" Li Bai and other outstanding poets, like towering and magnificent high mountains, exerted an indelible influence on the entire Han culture circle of East Asia. After the Tang

（4）书法绘画艺术

产生于中国黄河流域的独特象形文字——汉字，历史源远流长，是世界上流传至今的最为古老的文字体系。从 3500 余年前的商代甲骨文开始，即形成较为成熟的表达方式，经过西周金文、秦代篆文的发展完善，至汉代隶书的形成，文字外形、书写规则基本稳定，奠定了古汉字向现代汉字转化的基础，故称"隶变"。

自隶书开始，书法逐渐成为专门的书写艺术形式，自魏晋南北朝至隋唐时期，楷书、草书、行书等不同特色书法流派相继涌现，出现了如王羲之、欧阳询、颜真卿（图 3-19）、柳公权等一大批极具个人风格的杰出书法家。汉字及其书写艺术，逐渐传播至整个东亚地区，古代朝鲜、日本、越南、琉球等国家均把汉字作为官方文字，形成独具特色的东亚汉字文化圈。同汉字书法一样，古代中国绘画以其独特的绘画材料、艺术表现方式，展现出中华民族独有的审美情趣，成为世界艺术宝库的主要流派之一。不同于西方绘画，中国绘画以毛笔为主要工具，利用水

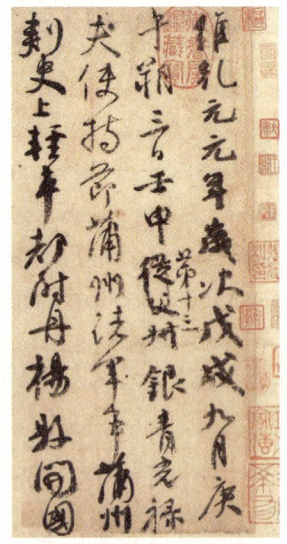

图 3-19　唐颜真卿书法名作《祭侄文稿》

Fig. 3-19　*Manuscript of Sacrifice to My Nephew*

A calligraphy masterpiece by Yan Zhenqing of the Tang Dynasty

Dynasty, Ci Poetry which originated from folk music yielded extraordinarily brilliant results in the Song Dynasty. Unlike "poetry expressing will" with grand narrative themes, Ci Poetry paid more attention to the expression of personal feelings which were delicate and graceful, lively and free as well, closely related to intensive development of the secular society, and witnessed another peak in the development of Chinese literature. Poetry of the Tang Dynasty is on a par with Ci Poetry of the Song Dynasty for the symbolic icons of Chinese literature and art, the typical representatives of the flourishing development of the Yellow River culture in the Tang and Song dynasties, and the common cultural sustenance and spiritual home of Chinese people in later generations.

(4) Calligraphy and Painting

The unique hieroglyphics—Chinese character, which originated in the Yellow River Basin, is the most ancient character writing system in the world with a long history. Oracle Bone Inscriptions in the Shang Dynasty developed to be a relatively mature way of expression more than 3,500 years ago, and further developed to be Inscriptions on Ancient Bronze Objects in the Western Zhou Dynasty and Seal Scripts in the Qin. Till the Han Dynasty, Official Script was set, with the basic stabilization of character shape and writing rules, which laid the foundation for the transformation of ancient Chinese characters into modern ones, giving it the name "Chinese Characters Evolution."

From Official Script, calligraphy gradually became a specialized art of writing. Since the Wei, Jin, Southern and Northern dynasties to the Sui and Tang dynasties, Regular Script, Cursive Script, Running Script and other schools of calligraphy emerged one after another. The most outstanding calligraphers were Wang Xizhi, Ouyang Xun, Yan Zhenqing (Fig. 3-19), Liu Gongquan and a large number of brilliant calligraphers who were known for pioneering their own styles. Chinese characters and their writing art gradually spread to the whole East Asia in which ancient Korea, Japan, Vietnam, Ryukyu and other countries all took Chinese characters as official characters, forming the East Asian cultural circle of Chinese characters with solitary characteristics. Like Chinese calligraphy, ancient Chinese painting, with its unique painting materials and artistic expression, showed the unique aesthetic taste of Chinese nation, and became one of the main schools of world treasury of arts. Unlike Western painting, Chinese painting took

祁连河谷 摄影/董保华
Qilian River Valley (photo by Dong Baohua)

writing brush as the main tool, used Chinese ink, cinnabar, blue stone and other mineral pigments, took lines as the main device of configuration, paid attention to implication and imagination space, and gradually co-opted and assimilated exotic artistic styles of the Western Regions, Yumen Pass and Central Asia. From the Han Dynasty to the Sui and Tang dynasties, Chinese painting gradually developed and matured, exerting a huge influence on East Asia and even the world.

(5) Religious Thought

Both Taoism and Buddhism had the greatest influence on ancient Chinese people. The former was the indigenous religion, and the latter the foreign one. They spread and developed in the Yellow River Basin, and rose to their peak from the Han to the Sui and Tang dynasties. Taoism in ancient China, on the ground of folk fairy beliefs and later depending on purposive Taoism, integrated divination from the Spring and Autumn Period, the Warring States Period to the Qin and Han dynasties. Taoist groups emerged at the end of the Eastern Han Dynasty, and till the Wei, Jin, and Southern and Northern dynasties, many schools were formed with a wealth of books and records. It was appointed as the State Religion during the Tang Dynasty—the heyday of its development.

Buddhism originated from India and was introduced into China during the Eastern Han Dynasty. The existing White Horse Temple (Fig. 3-20) in Luoyang of Henan Province is the oldest Buddhist temple in China. It was built during the reign of Emperor Mingdi of the Eastern Han Dynasty. Buddhism was characterized by its subtle secret which was full of speculation about the meaning of life and ultimate concern for life and death, which to a certain extent, made up for the lack of exploring the world origin of philosophy ontology in early Confucianism and indigenous religions in China. Therefore, once Buddhism was introduced into China, it spread rapidly in the Wei, Jin and Southern and Northern dynasties, with its adherents, temples and Buddhist statues all over the country.

By the Tang Dynasty, the doctrines and theories of Buddhism had grown and matured in China, developing into eight important sects, including Faxiang, Tiantai, Lü, Jingtu and Chan (Zen). They also began the evolution from simple learning to localized creation. Sinicized Buddhism represented by Chan (Zen) gradually became the mainstream in later generations.

墨及朱砂、青石等矿物颜料,以线条为主要构型手段,注重意蕴想象空间,并逐渐借鉴吸收西域、玉门关、中亚等地的域外艺术风格,在两汉至隋唐时期逐渐发展成熟,对东亚地区乃至世界产生了巨大的影响。

(5)宗教思想

对古代中国民众影响最深的两大宗教,当属道教与佛教,一为本土宗教,一为外来宗教,在两汉至隋唐时期的黄河流域得以传播发展、趋于鼎盛。道教以中国古老的民间原始神仙信仰为基础,后以黄老道家思想为依托,整合春秋战国、秦汉以来的修仙方术,在东汉末年出现有组织的道教团体,至魏晋南北朝时期形成众多流派和丰富的道教典籍,到唐代道教被定为国教,发展最为鼎盛。

佛教源自印度,在东汉时期传入中国,现存河南洛阳的佛教名刹"白马寺"(图3-20)即兴建于东汉明帝时期,为中国最古老的佛寺。佛教以其教义精奥,饱含对人生意义的思辨、对生死问题的终极关怀等特点,在一定程度上可以弥补中国早期儒家和本土宗教缺乏探究世界本源方面哲学本体论的不足,故一经传入中国,即在魏晋南北朝时期得到迅速的传播,信徒广众,寺院伽蓝、佛教造像遍布全国。

至唐代,佛教教义理论在中国发展成熟,形成法相宗、天台宗、律宗、净土宗、禅宗等八个重要派别,也开始实现由单纯学习到本土化创造的转变,以禅宗为代表的中国化佛教在后世逐渐占据主流地位。

与基督教、伊斯兰教等世界其他主要宗教不同,道教与佛教在中国传播的最主要特色,体现在宗教神权最终屈从服务于世俗政权,神职宗教领袖及其机构隶属于中央官僚体制,这与中国早期集权制封建王朝以现实理性的儒家思想为治国根本、以黄河流域为中心的世俗官僚体系的强大治理管控能力有密切的关系。中国的道教、佛教,经过汉代至唐代与儒家思想长期的分歧争论,最终实现互相借鉴融合,形成三教合流的独特现象,其宗教思想和流派逐渐传播至东亚、东南亚等地区,并对当地政治、文化产生了持久而重要的影响。

Unlike other major religions in the world such as Christianity and Islam, the key features of Taoism and Buddhism spreading in China embodied the final submission of religious theocracy to secular regime, and subordination of holy religious leaders and their institutions to the central bureaucracy. It was closely related to the powerful governance and control of secular bureaucracy in the early centralized feudal dynasties of China which were centered on the Yellow River Basin and based on the realistic and rational Confucianism. Taoism and Buddhism in China, after a long period of disagreement with and debate against Confucianism during the Han and Tang dynasties, finally realized reference and fusion, forming a unique converging phenomenon of the three religions. Their religious thoughts and schools gradually spread to other regions in East Asia and Southeast Asia, and exerted a lasting and important influence on local politics and culture.

图 3-20 洛阳白马寺

Fig. 3-20 White Horse Temple in Luoyang City

三、分久必合：多民族统一国家的壮大与发展

推崇统一、强调融合是中国历代以来的政治文化传统，战国时代的《春秋公羊传》即推崇"大一统"之说，主要包含三个层面的内涵，即"尊王"为核心的政治一统、"华夏"为核心的民族一统和"礼乐"为核心的文化一统。"大一统"观念逐渐成为中国文化阶层的政治共识和最高追求，形成秉持兼容、开拓精神的天下观；大一统体制有利于维持封建时代社会的相对稳定性，降低分裂带来的潜在动荡风险，也使中国境内各民族视统一为正常状态、分裂为非常状态成为一种共同的心理认知。而中国多民族统一国家奠基时代在西周至秦汉时期，其核心区域正在黄河中下游的广袤农耕文化地区。

1. 以黄河流域为核心的大一统帝国形成

（1）秦、汉帝国

秦、汉帝国的相继崛起为中国多民族大一统帝国的形成奠定了基础。秦都咸阳，汉代以长安、洛阳为两京，继承了自西周以来华夏部族以渭河、洛河流域为政治核心的传统格局。秦、汉帝国可以说是中华文明的青年时代，充满孔武有力、飞扬进取的阳刚、乐观气息。秦国一统中国，北至辽东、南抵南海，书同文而车同轨，废分封而行郡县，制度多开创之举，故后世有"百代皆行秦制"之言，现今欧洲有称中国"China"源自于"秦"之说。汉承秦制，而国祚长久，独尊儒术，国力富强，开疆拓土（图3-21），凿空西域，在国际舞台上大放异彩。汉代最突出的历史贡献还在于：在长期稳定整合、区域交流频繁的背景下，汉王朝以黄河流域周、秦文化为核心，融合长江流域楚、吴越文化，使得具有共同礼仪文化、民族认同的主体民族——汉族最终形成，开启了中国以汉族为主体的多民族国家政权构建新时代。

III. Unifications and Divisions: the Growth and Development of a Multi-ethnic Unified Country

Advocating unity and emphasizing integration have been the political and cultural traditions of China since ancient times. *Gongyang's Spring and Autumn Annals* in the Warring States Period praised highly the theory of "Great Unification," which mainly contained three levels, namely, political unification, national unification and cultural unification with the "king," "Huaxia" and "rites and music" as the core respectively. "Great Unification" gradually became the political consensus and noblest pursuit of the Chinese academic stratum, forming a world view that upheld the spirit of compatibility and pioneering. The unified system was conducive to maintaining the relative stability of the feudal society and reducing the potential risks of turbulence caused by division. It also made it a common psychological cognition that all ethnic groups in China regarded unification as a normal state and division as an abnormal one. However, the foundation of China's multi-ethnic unified country was laid from the Western Zhou Dynasty (1046-771 BC) to the Qin (221-206 BC) and Han dynasties (206 BC-220 AD). And its core area was the vast farming culture region in the middle and lower reaches of the Yellow River.

1. The Formation of a Unified Empire with the Yellow River Basin at the Core

(1) Qin and Han empires

The successive rise of the Qin and Han empires laid a foundation for the formation of the unified multi-ethnic empire of China. The Qin Dynasty took Xianyang and the Han Dynasty took Chang'an and Luoyang as their capitals, inheriting the traditional pattern composition that the Chinese tribes had taken the Weihe River and the Luohe River basins as the political core since the Western Zhou Dynasty. The Qin and Han empires can be said to be the youth of Chinese civilization, vigorous, enterprising and optimistic. The State of Qin unified China, reaching Liaodong in the north and the South China Sea in the south. It stipulated the use of standard characters and unified ruts, abolished the system of enfeoffment and implemented the system of prefectures. Its system was

图 3-21 西汉时期全图

谭其骧:《中国历史地图集》,中国地图出版社,1982 年版

Fig. 3-21 Full picture of the Western Han Dynasty

Tan Qixiang: *Chinese Historical Atlas*, China Cartographic Publishing House, 1982 edition

(2)隋、唐帝国

继秦、汉帝国之后,经过魏晋南北朝时期的分裂动乱,汉族文明与北方少数民族文明经过长时间的纷争与相互借鉴,隋、唐帝国接踵而起,以开放多元、强盛自信闻名于世。尤其是唐王朝,疆域北达蒙古高原、南至中南半岛、西及中亚地区(图3-22),达到中国政治版图顶峰,四方异域国家政治、贸易往来不绝,堪称世界级大国。唐代的政治制度、经济、文化,乃至宗教、艺术等各方面,均带有明显的盛世色彩,不拘一格,外向自信,为后世所缅怀景仰,尊称其为"盛唐气象"。

隋、唐帝国建立在北魏鲜卑族政权的基础之上,其核心政治集团——关陇集团,融合了鲜卑及汉族贵族势力。而关陇集团形成的政治背景,与北魏孝文帝开启的主动汉化、积极向华夏文明学习的过程息息相关。隋、唐帝国的伟大文明成就,是华夏黄河文明与北方异族文明融合混血

mostly pioneering, so the later generations said that "all generations had followed the Qin system." Today, there is a view in Europe that "China" originated from the Qin Dynasty. The Han Dynasty followed the Qin system, and the country lasted for a long time. The flourishing country, with its exclusive worship for Confucianism, its expansion of territory, and its connection with the Western Regions (a Han Dynasty term for the area west of Yumenguan, including what is now Xinjiang and parts of Central Asia) (Fig. 3-21), made itself shine brilliantly on the international arena. The most prominent historical contribution of the Han Dynasty also lied in: with long-term stable integration and frequent regional exchanges, the Han Dynasty centered on Zhou and Qin cultures in the Yellow River Basin, and integrated Chu and Wuyue cultures in the Yangtze River Basin, resulting in the formation of the Han nationality, the main ethnic group with common etiquette culture and national identity. The new era of China's multi-ethnic state power construction with the Han nationality as the main body has begun.

(2) Sui and Tang empires

Following the Qin and Han dynasties, after the division and turmoil in the Wei, Jin, Southern and Northern dynasties, the Han civilization and the northern minority civilizations underwent long disputes and combinations. Then Sui and Tang empires rose and they were famous for their openness, diversity, strength and confidence. The Tang Empire, in particular, reached the Mongolian Plateau in the north, Indochina Peninsula in the south, and Central Asia in the west (Fig. 3-22), attaining the peak of China's political landscape. It had endless political and trade exchanges with surrounding countries, being a world-class power. The political system, economy, culture, religion, art and other aspects of the Tang Dynasty (618-907 AD) were all characterized by prosperity, being eclectic and confident. The Tang Dynasty was remembered and respected by posterity, and was honored as "The Flourishing Tang Dynasty."

The Sui and Tang empires were established on the basis of the Northern Wei Dynasty (386-534 AD) of the Xianbei nationality. Its core political group, the Guanlong Group, integrated the Xianbei and Han aristocratic forces. The political background of the formation of the Guanlong Group was closely related to the process of active Chinesization reform and the learning from Chinese civilization

图 3-22　唐时期全图

谭其骧：《中国历史地图集》，中国地图出版社，1982 年版

Fig. 3-22　Full picture of the Tang Dynasty

Tan Qixiang: *Chinese Historical Atlas*, China Cartographic Publishing House, 1982 edition

后所绽放出的灿烂之花，一改东汉末年至魏晋时期汉族士大夫文化的内向、颓靡之风，焕发出新的勃勃生机，是黄河文明海纳百川、开放包容特质的典型体现。

2. 以黄河文明为主流的文化传播与扩散

（1）礼乐正统观念的形成

礼乐制度形成、完善于西周时期。史载周公旦"制礼作乐"，为礼乐制度始创者。礼乐制度与宗法制、分封制共同构成了西周封建等级社会的基础。春秋时期孔子以周公创制的西周社会文明为正统，对礼乐制度重新进行系统阐释和理论化构建。孔子所主张的礼乐文化包含了维护社会秩序的政治制度构建，实现家庭、宗族和谐的伦理思想以及提升个人认知水平的修身理念。儒家思想认为"礼"是代表天地万物、社会运

initiated by Emperor Xiaowen of the Northern Wei Dynasty. The great civilization achievements of the Sui and Tang empires were the brilliant flowers blooming after the integration of the Yellow River civilization of China and the alien civilization of the north. They changed the introversion and decadence of the Han literati culture from the late Eastern Han Dynasty to the Wei and Jin dynasties (265-420 AD), and brimmed with dynamism, typically reflecting the characteristics of the Yellow River civilization, which was open and inclusive.

2. Cultural Dissemination and Diffusion with the Yellow River Civilization as the Mainstream

(1) The formation of orthodox ideas of rites and music

The rites and music system was formed and perfected in the Western Zhou Dynasty. According to the historical records, Duke of Zhou, who was named Dan, the founder of the rites and music system, "created rites for music." The rites and music system, the patriarchal clan system and the system of enfeoffment together formed the foundation of the feudal hierarchical society in the Western Zhou Dynasty. During the Spring and Autumn Period, Confucius took the social civilization of the Western Zhou Dynasty created by the Duke of Zhou as orthodoxy and reinterpreted and theorized the rites and music system. The rites and music culture advocated by Confucius included the construction of political system to maintain social order, the ethical thought of realizing family and clan harmony, and the cultivation of morality to improve self-cognitive capacities. Confucianism believed that "rite" was the "reason" that represented the laws of all the things in the world and the operation of society, "formulated ritual as a criterion to standardize the relationship between monarch and minister, and to render the relationship between father and son honest, the relationship among brothers amicable, and the relationship between husband and wife harmonious" (Fig. 3-23), and also "the so-called music was moderation." "Music" was to be restrained, to be "joyous but not indecent, mournful but not distressing," and to be the impartial Golden Mean. The rites and music system required "a gentleman did things neither without reason nor without restraint," which became a social norm at the national level and a code of conduct at the individual level. It also became an important symbol that distinguished the Chinese orthodox civilization from

转规律的"理","以正君臣,以笃父子,以睦兄弟,以和夫妇"(图3-23),而"乐也者,节也"。"乐"是要节制有度,做到"乐而不淫,哀而不伤",要做到不偏不倚、中庸有道。礼乐制度要求"无理不动,无节不作",成为国家层面的社会规范和个人层次的行为准则,也成为华夏正统文明区别于周边其他"蛮夷"的重要标志。

随着汉代以来儒家思想主导地位的确立,礼乐制度逐渐成为博大精深的华夏文化体系中的核心元素,在后世衍化为代表正统中原文明的象征性符号,成为具有基因标志作用的古老黄河文化代表和华夏族群身份象征,亦成为历代封建王朝宣示、构建政权合法性的光辉旗帜,延绵千年而不绝。

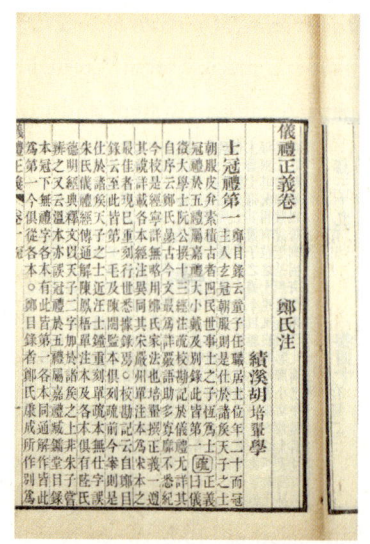

图 3-23 清刻本《仪礼正义》
Fig. 3-23 The Qing block-printed edition of *Rites*

(2)儒家文化与教化推广

中国古代传统儒家特别重视教育的作用,强调"有教无类"的包容精神。儒家经典《易经》即提出"关乎人文,以化成天下"之说,

other neighboring "barbarians."

With the establishment of the dominant position of Confucianism since the Han Dynasty, rites and music system gradually became a core element in the extensive and profound Chinese cultural system. In later generations, it evolved into a symbolic sign representing the orthodox Central Plains civilization and became a representative of the ancient Yellow River culture with the functions of a genetic marker and a symbol of the identity of the Chinese ethnic group, and also became a glorious banner for feudal dynasties to declare and build the legitimacy of the regime, lasting for thousands of years.

(2) Confucianism and Its Promotion

The traditional Confucianism in ancient China attached great importance to education, emphasizing the inclusiveness of "education for all without discrimination." The Confucian classic *The Book of Changes* stated that "looking at the civilized etiquette of human society can educate the world" and advocated the ultimate goal of a pacific society through the promotion of etiquette culture. Since the Western Han Dynasty which established the general plan of the government of "paying supreme tribute to Confucianism," being familiar with Confucian classical culture gradually became the primary condition for the central government to appoint local officials. As active supporters of Confucianism, the bureaucratic intellectuals shouldered the lofty mission of spreading Confucian culture and etiquette throughout the country. The "upright officials," who were frequently seen in historical books, commended by the court and praised by the people (Fig. 3-24), were representatives of outstanding local officials who actively promoted Confucianism in the localities and borders. They spread the advanced production technology and culture of the Central Plains to all corners of China, restricting local social customs such as sacrifice, marriage and funeral with Confucian ritual system, and praising local people for practicing ethics. They established schools, set up supervision, assessment and selection systems, and actively promoted Confucian culture and education. With the gradual expansion of the political landscape of the Han and Tang empires, Confucian culture gradually spread from the core area of the Yellow River Basin to the entire East Asia. In the Tang and Song dynasties, with the development of the imperial examination system, the trend of popularization of education became more and

主张通过礼仪文化的推广达到天下大治的终极目标。自西汉确立"独尊儒术"的治国方略之后，熟知儒家经典文化逐渐成为中央政府任命地方官员的首要条件，官僚知识阶层作为儒家思想的积极拥护者，担负起在全国各地传播儒家文化、礼制的崇高使命。屡屡见于史书、受到朝廷表彰和民众称赞的"循吏"（图3-24），即是积极在地方和边疆推行儒家教化的优秀地方官员代表。他们把中原地区的先进生产技术和文化传播至中国的各个角落，以儒家礼制约束地方的祭祀、婚姻、丧葬等社会风俗，旌表地方民众践行儒家伦理道德。建立学校，设定督导、考核、选拔制度，积极推广儒家文化教育。随着汉、唐王朝政治版图的逐步扩大，儒家文化从核心区域黄河流域逐渐扩散至整个东亚地区。至唐、宋时期，随着科举制度发展，教育平民化趋势越来越明显，使得儒家文化在社会各阶层的渗透传播更加深入，儒家思想成为上至国家政治意识，下至宗族家庭伦理、平民生活习俗所严格遵循的指导准则。

3. 以中原地区汉族为主体的民族认同确立

（1）华夏与蛮夷认知

现代中华民族多元一体的民族共同体的形成，经历了悠久漫长的发展过程，其演变历程充分展现了中国古老黄河文化的多元、包容性格。春秋时代，以黄河中下游地区为主要活动范围的"华夏族"逐步形成，并产生"华夏"与"蛮夷"相区分的民族意识，强调天下以"华夏"为文明中心，视四周"蛮夷"为从属。这种认知固然有其时代的局限性，但对中国古代中原地区的民族认同凝聚亦产生了积极的作用，对后世以黄河流域稳定的主体族群——汉族的形成产生了决定性的影响。

而且不同于现代西方国家对民族的硬性区分，古代中国的"华夷"思想是以"礼"分群的文化族类观，更强调族群的文化认同属性，若"蛮夷"采用了华夏礼制，则即为华夏族，充满包容弹性。而且自孔子时代即逐步发展出"四海之内皆兄弟"的"华夷一统观"，强调"天

more evident, which made the penetration and dissemination of Confucian culture in all the strata of society more in-depth. Confucianism became the guiding principle strictly followed by the national political consciousness, the clan family ethics and the common people's living customs.

图3-24 西汉著名循吏——黄霸像

Fig. 3-24 The statue of the famous upright official in the Western Han Dynasty—Huang Ba

3. Establishment of Ethnic Identity with Han Nationality as the Main Body in Central Plains Region

(1) Cognition of Huaxia and Barbarians

The formation of the pluralistic and integrated national community of the modern Chinese nation has developed for a long history, demonstrating the diverse and inclusive characters of the Chinese ancient Yellow River culture. During the Spring and Autumn Period, the "Huaxia" with the middle and lower reaches of the Yellow River as the main scope of activities gradually formed, and the national consciousness of distinguishing between "Huaxia" and "barbarians" came into being, emphasizing that the world took "Huaxia" as the center of civilization and the surrounding "barbarians" as subordinates. Although this kind of cognition had its limitations in times, it also played a positive role in rallying national identity in the Central Plains in ancient China. It exerted a decisive influence on the formation of the later Han nationality, the main ethnic group stabilized in the Yellow River Basin.

图3-25　唐高宗乾陵六十一蕃臣像

Fig. 3-25　The sixty-one statues of Tibetan officials in Qianling Mausoleum of Emperor Gaozong of the Tang Dynasty

下共主、抚有四海"的大一统理念，为汉、唐王朝包容异族的"天下"意识形成奠定了基础（图3-25），充满开放、自信的强盛气魄。

（2）羁縻与同化策略

中国古代的治辖理念以周代形成的向心式"五服"天下体系认知为典型代表。《尚书·禹贡》划分"五服"为甸服、侯服、绥服、要服、荒服，以王都为中心，每隔五百里为一等级，区分不同的治理方式和礼制要求（图3-26）。"五服"之制虽然具有明显的理想化色彩，但

四川唐克的黄河 摄影/董保华
The Yellow River in Tangke Village, Sichuan Province (photo by Dong Baohua)

对后世大一统帝国的民族事务治理提供了重要准则。对帝国边疆的少数民族，统治手段相对温和，很少采取过激的同化政策，而是在威服的基础上采取间接治理的策略，通过羁縻政策和渐进涓滴的文化渗透，使得中原地区的文化逐渐为周边民族所主动接受。正是这种主要依靠文化吸引而非绝对武力强制的辐射同化政策，对古代中国以中原地区汉族为核心、多民族交流共存的民族格局形成产生了深远的影响，对现代中华民族共同体的和谐构建和最终定型起到了积极的推动作用。

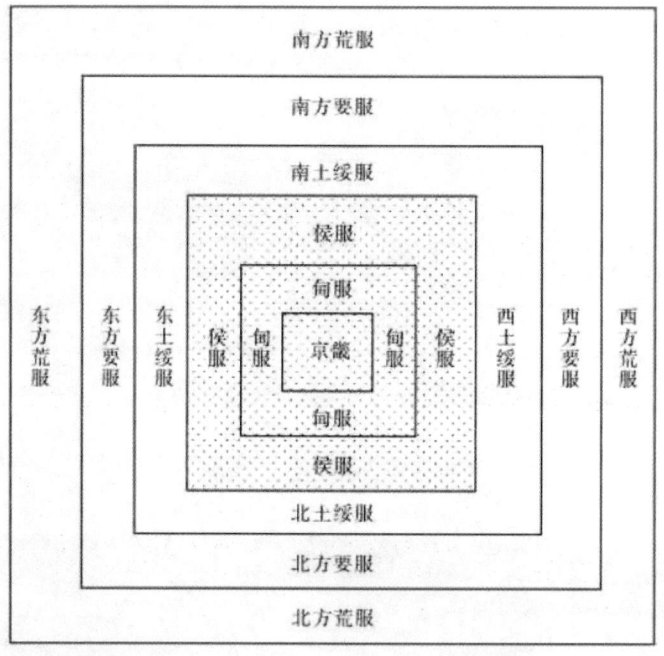

图3-26 西周传统礼制——五服之制示意图

Fig. 3-26 Schematic diagram of traditional ritual system in the Western Zhou Dynasty—"Wufu" system

Moreover, different from the rigid distinction of ethnic groups in modern Western countries, the ancient Chinese thought of "the Han people and the minorities" was a cultural ethnic view that divided groups by "ritual," which emphasized the cultural identity of ethnic groups. If the "barbarians" adopted the Chinese ritual system, they joined the Huaxia people. This viewpoint was comprehensive and resilient. Moreover, since the Confucius' time, the "unified view of the Han people and the minorities" of "all men under heaven were brothers" gradually developed, emphasizing the unified concept of "the emperor under heaven administered the whole earth." This laid the foundation for the formation of the "all under heaven" consciousness of the Han and Tang empires that tolerated alien races (Fig. 3-25). It was full of openness, confidence and prosperity.

(2) Mollification and Assimilation Strategy

The concept of governance in ancient China was typically represented by the centripetal "Wufu" under-heaven system cognition formed in the Zhou Dynasty (1046-256 BC). According to *Book of History*, the system of "Wufu" included Dianfu, Houfu, Suifu, Yaofu, and Huangfu. The division of "Wufu" was centered on the capital of the king, with a grade every 500 li (equal to 155 miles), and distinguished different governance patterns and ritual requirements (Fig. 3-26). Although "Wufu" system was obviously idealized, it provided important guidelines for the governance of ethnic affairs in the later unified empires. For the ethnic minorities in the imperial frontier, the ruling method of the empires was relatively liberal with rare adoption of extreme assimilation policies. Instead, it adopted indirect governance on the basis of threat. Through mollification policy and gradual cultural infiltration, the culture of the Central Plains was gradually embraced by neighboring ethnic groups. It was this radiating assimilation policy, which mainly relied on cultural attraction rather than absolute force, that had a far-reaching impact on the formation of the ethnic pattern in ancient China, with the Han nationality in the Central Plains as the core and different ethnics communicating and coexisting, and played a positive role in promoting the harmonious construction and finally shaping the modern Chinese national community.

第四章

熔铸与再生：奔流到海不复回

Chapter 4

Fusion and Revival: an Irreversible Trend

一、开枝散叶：黄河文化的北移南徙

夏、商、周时代早期黄河文化的核心，位于黄河中游晋南、豫西、豫北交界区域，司马迁《史记》称为"三河天下中"（河东、河南、河内），是"中国"概念的发源地。随着西周礼乐文明、宗法制度的定型，以及其后秦、汉、唐等大一统帝国的形成和地理疆域的拓展，成熟而发达的黄河文化逐步开枝散叶，涓滴渗透，不断向南、向北辐射扩散，同化吸收异质文化，为一核多元的中华民族共同体形成、壮大奠定了稳固的基础。

1. 黄河文化的北移

（1）箕子朝鲜的建立

箕子，殷商末年著名贤臣，商纣王之叔父，与比干、微子并称殷"三仁"（图4-1）。商纣王暴虐，比干因谏被杀，微子被迫装疯为奴。周武王灭商后，箕子率殷遗民入朝鲜，建立箕子朝鲜。

图4-1　河南淇县祭祀箕子之三仁祠

Fig. 4–1　The Temple of the Three Benevolent Saints in honor of Jizi in Qi County, Henan Province

Ⅰ. The Northward and Southward Spread of the Yellow River Culture

The core of the early Yellow River culture in dynasties of Xia, Shang and Zhou lied at the intersection of the south of Shanxi, the west of Henan and the north of Henan in the middle reaches of the Yellow River, where the concept of "China" originated. With the stereotyping of the rite-music civilization and the patriarch system of the Western Zhou Dynasty, and the subsequent formulation of the unified empires of Qin, Han and Tang and the resulting territorial expansion, the mature and developed Yellow River culture gradually flourished, filtrated and continually spread both to the south and the north, assimilated the heterogenous cultures, and eventually laid a solid foundation for the formulation and growth of one-core- multiple-elements Chinese national community.

1.The Northward Movement of the Yellow River Culture

(1) The Foundation of Jizi Korea

Jizi, a famous competent official of the late Shang Dynasty, also the uncle of the King Zhou, was collectively called the "Three Benevolent Saints" with Bigan and Weizi (Fig. 4-1). The King Zhou was ruthless, Bigan was beheaded after offering a piece of advice, and Weizi was forced to feign madness and became a slave. After the King Wu annihilated the Shang Dynasty, Jizi led the remaining civilians eastward and established Jizi Korea.

According to *The Book of Han*, "The Shang Dynasty declined, Jizi left his homeland and went to Korea, and taught the inhabitants there how to behave properly and how to raise the silkworm and weave." Jizi spread the advanced agricultural civilization to the Korean Peninsula, improved the local productive force, implemented the law of eight articles, made the local inhabitants behave properly with the Chinese civilization of rites, forbad the inhabitants to kill randomly or steal, laid down the regulations for marriage and funeral, and the results in Korea were: there were no thieves or bandits, the local people held good faith in high esteem, and people could leave their door open without worrying about the appearance of robbers.

《汉书·地理志》记载，"殷道衰，箕子去之朝鲜，教其民以礼义，田蚕织作"，把黄河流域先进的农耕文明推行到朝鲜半岛，提高当地物质生产力水平。推行"八条之教"，以中国礼制文明教化当地百姓，禁止民众擅杀、偷盗，制定婚丧嫁娶礼仪，使得朝鲜民无盗贼，崇尚信义，夜不闭户，民风淳朴。

箕子朝鲜在朝鲜历史上享有很高的声誉，开启朝鲜半岛吸收中原黄河文明成果的先河。后世朝鲜王朝对箕子朝鲜的认同，正是其学习、接受华夏文明的根源。箕子是朝鲜文明建设的英雄人物，也是中国历史上忠义精神的代表，一直作为先贤楷模被后世崇敬。至今位于河南淇县的"三仁庙"犹保存完好，为历代王朝供奉祭祀箕子之所，香火不绝。

（2）匈奴归降与同化

匈奴是古代中国北方著名的游牧民族，据司马迁《史记·匈奴列传》所载，其先祖是华夏民族夏后氏之一支，于夏末商初北迁，世代游牧为生。在秦、汉之际兴起于阴山山脉，称雄一时，屡为中国之患。秦始皇统一中国后，派遣蒙恬将匈奴逐出黄河中上游之河西走廊和河套地区，并修筑长城以固守。西汉武帝至元帝时期，在汉军的屡次打击下，匈奴内部逐渐分裂。汉元帝时期，南匈奴单于呼韩邪归降，并请和亲于汉朝，以女婿相称，汉朝将王昭君嫁给呼韩邪单于，是为著名的"昭君出塞"。

西汉与匈奴维持了长时期的和平与物质、文化交流，黄河文明逐渐渗透扩散至塞北地区，开启了匈奴汉化的历史进程。其中最为著名的是南匈奴休屠王太子金日䃅（图4-2），其人深受汉武帝信任，被赐汉姓封侯，受遗诏成为汉昭帝之辅政大臣。金日䃅是西汉历史上著名的少数民族政治家，其子孙亦皆以恪守儒家忠孝礼节而成为美谈。

东汉时期，匈奴再次分裂为南、北匈奴，南匈奴率先归附，被光武帝安置在河套地区。汉和帝时期名将窦宪大败北匈奴于燕然山，勒石记功而还，自此北匈奴远遁中亚草原。南匈奴逐渐被汉族同化，改汉姓，遵汉俗。在西晋灭亡后的"五胡乱华"时期，南匈奴首领刘渊建立"前

Jizi Korea enjoyed a high reputation in the Korean history, and it initiated the absorption of the outcome of the Central Plains Yellow River civilization by the Korean Peninsula. The later Korean dynasties identified with Jizi Korea, and it was the reason why it learned and accepted the Huaxia civilization. Jizi was a hero since he greatly contributed to the promotion of the Korean civilization, and he was also the leading exponent of the spirit of loyalty and faith in the Chinese history. Jizi has since been held in high esteem by later generations. The Temple of the Three Benevolent Saints has been preserved perfectly even by now, and it has been continuously adorned by successive dynasties.

(2) The Surrender and Assimilation of the Huns

The Huns were famous nomadic tribes in the north of ancient China. According to Sima Qian's "Biography of Huns" in *The Historical Records*, their ancestors were a branch of Xiahoushi of the Huaxia nationality, and they migrated northward at the end of the Xia Dynasty and the early of the Shang Dynasty, and lived by nomadism. And they flourished in the Yinshan Mountains between the decline of the Qin Dynasty and the rise of the Han Dynasty, posing a great threat to China for a long period of time. After the First Emperor of the Qin Dynasty realized the unification of China, he sent Meng Tian to dispel the Huns from the middle and upper reaches of the Yellow River, and built the Great Wall to defend them. In the Dynasty of Western Han between the Emperor Wu and the Emperor Yuan, the Huns split as a result of successive attacks by the Han troops. At the time of the reign of the Emperor Yuan, the leader of the southern Huns surrendered, and asked for a proposal as the son-in-law with the Han Dynasty, and Wang Zhaojun was accordingly married to him by the arrangement of the Han Dynasty, which was called "Zhaojun going beyond the Great Wall."

The Western Han Dynasty long maintained with the Huns peace and the intercourse of material and culture, and the Yellow River civilization gradually infiltrated and spread to the north beyond the Great Wall, which initiated the process of integration of the Huns with the Han nationality. A very famous case in point was about the Prince of Jin Midi of the south Huns. He was deeply trusted by the Emperor Wu, was created the nobility within the system of the Han Dynasty, and was appointed the Advisory Lord of the Emperor Zhao in accordance with the decree of the dying Emperor Wu on his deathbed. Jinmidi

图4-2　汉武帝茂陵陪葬墓——金日磾墓（陕西省兴平市）
Fig. 4-2 Jin Midi Tomb (Xingping City, Shaanxi Province)

赵"政权，国号为"汉"，以汉朝正统自居，南匈奴族群融入北方汉族群体之中，渐渐同化于以汉族为主体的历史进程之中。

（3）北魏鲜卑族之汉化

鲜卑族起源于大兴安岭北部区域，其分支拓跋部不断游牧南迁，在西晋末年活跃于今晋北地区，于公元 439 年逐步统一中国北方，结束了西晋汉族政权灭亡后"五胡乱华"的动荡割据局面，史称北魏。

北魏历代君主多仰慕黄河中下游地区先进的汉族文明，并与当地汉族士大夫联姻。孝文帝拓跋宏，由汉族出身的冯太后抚养长大，受汉文化熏陶极深，实施了全面汉化的改革措施，把首都由北方平城（今山西大同）迁至黄河流域腹地洛阳（图4-3）；禁胡语而说汉语，改鲜卑姓为汉姓，鼓励上层官僚与汉族通婚；采用秦汉以来的中央集权官僚制度和赋税体制。这些措施，大大促进了中国北方地区的民族融合和互相交流，北方少数民族吸收了以汉族为主体的黄河文明物质、文化精华，大大促进了农业生产的进步和社会的稳定，黄河文明亦吸收了异族文明的新鲜血液，进一步焕发生机活力，为中华民族的融合发展做出了伟大的贡献，也给此后隋、唐大一统帝国的形成奠定了良好的基础。

was a famous politician of minority nationality in the history of the Western Han Dynasty, and his offspring all complied with the Confucian morality and continuously enjoyed a good reputation.

In the Eastern Han Dynasty, the Huns split again into the north tribes and the south tribes. The south tribes took the lead in surrendering, and were allowed to live in the Hetao areas. At the reign of the Emperor He, the famous general Dou Xian defeated the north tribes in the Mountain of Yanran, and carved on the cliff of the mountain an aphorism to boast their great victory before they returned. The north tribes then fled faraway to the Central Asian grassland. The south tribes became gradually assimilated by the Han nationality, and they used the Han surnames and followed the Han rituals and customs. In the period of "Five Barbarians Invading China" after the fall of the Dynasty of Western Jin, Liu Yuan, the leader of the south tribes, established the ruling power of "Pre-Zhao," and they called the country "Han" to boast the direct lineage of the Han Dynasty. The south tribes were gradually integrated into the groups of the Han nationality in the north in the process of history.

(3) Xianbei Nationality's Modelling on Han Nationality in the Northern Wei Dynasty

The Xianbei nationality originated in the north of the Greater Khingan Mountains range, and Tuoba tribes as its branches continuously migrated southward as a result of nomadic reasons. At the end of the Western Jin Dynasty, they flourished in the north of today's Shanxi Province, and in 439 AD they gradually unified the north of China, putting an end to the turbulence caused by the so-called historical incident "Five Barbarians Invading China" after the fall of the Western Jin, and the dynasty they established was called Northern Wei.

The successive monarchs of the Northern Wei Dynasty mostly adorned the advanced civilization of the Han nationality in the regions along the middle and lower reaches of the Yellow River, and they proposed marriage with the local high officials of the Han nationality. The Emperor Xiaowen—Tuoba Hong, who was raised by the Queen Mother Feng of the Han descendent and deeply influenced by the Han culture, carried out the reform measures to realize the full-scale Hanization. He moved the capital from Pingcheng (today's Datong, Shanxi Province) in the north to Luoyang in the hinterland of the reaches of the

图4-3　北魏孝文帝礼佛图（洛阳龙门石窟石雕）

Fig. 4-3　Paying tribute to Buddha by the Emperor Xiaowen of the Northern Wei Dynasty (Longmen Grottos of Luoyang)

2. 黄河文化的南徙

（1）问鼎中原：黄河文化在长江流域的扩张

长江流域的楚国是春秋战国时期重要的政治力量，史籍记载楚人源自黄河流域的黄帝部落，在商、周之际从北方迁徙至汉水流域的"丹阳"（今河南淅川县境内），受到西周王朝的册封承认。这是楚人首次自中原进入湖北省内，也是楚国首次得到周王室的正式承认。楚国通过不断地向长江流域东、南方征伐兼并，"地方五千里"，战国时期成为疆域最大之诸侯国，境域横跨今湖北、湖南、安徽、江苏、河南、江西诸省。楚国虽然被北方中原黄河流域诸国视为南蛮而遭到轻视，但其始终以周天子封臣身份开拓疆土，遵守宗周礼法制度并不定期地朝贡，融合同化南方诸民族，使楚国文化充满生机和活力，亦间接地使中原黄河文明向长江流域不断扩散传播。公元前607年，楚庄王北伐至东周首都洛阳附近，举行阅兵仪式。周定王派使臣王孙满前去慰劳，楚庄王径直

Yellow River (Fig. 4-3). He forbad the speaking of the barbarian native languages and promoted the speaking of Chinese, changed the Xianbei surnames into the Han surnames, encouraged the intermarriage between the high officials and the Han inhabitants, and adopted the bureaucracy and fiscal systems adopted since the Qin and Han dynasties. All these measures greatly promoted the fusion and intercommunication between the nationalities of the North China. The minority nationalities of the North absorbed the material and cultural essence of the Yellow River civilization developed mainly by the Han nationality, and hence vastly promoted the progress of the agricultural production and the stability of the society; whereas on the other hand, the Yellow River civilization also assimilated the fresh elements of the civilization of other nationalities, revived furthermore, and contributed greatly to the fusion of the Chinese nationalities, laying a good foundation for the subsequent unified empires of Sui and Tang.

2. The Southward Spread of the Yellow River Culture

(1) Asking about the Weight of Tripod Ding in the Central Plains: the Expansion of the Yellow River Culture in the Yangtze River Reaches

The State of Chu in the Yangtze River reaches was an important political power in the Spring and Autumn Period and the Warring States Period. The historical books traced the ancestors of Chu back to the Huangdi tribes in the Yellow River reaches, and later in the dynasties between Shang and Zhou, their ancestors migrated from the North to "Danyang" (today's Xichuan County, Henan Province), and they were acknowledged by the Western Zhou Dynasty. It was the first time that the Chu people entered Hubei Province, and it was also the first time that the State of Chu obtained the official acknowledgement by the Zhou Dynasty. The State of Chu incessantly waged war on the eastern and southern reaches of the Yangtze river, annexed small countries, and had a large territorial area like a rectangle with a line length of five thousand li (a length unit, equal to 500 meters), becoming the largest vassal state in its size, covering areas in today's Hubei, Hunan, Anhui, Jiangsu, Henan, Jiangxi, and other provinces. The State of Chu was considered as a barbarian state and ignored by the North states of the Yellow River reaches, but it consistently enlarged the territory as the feudal vassal of the Zhou Son of Heaven, obeyed the rites and laws of the Zhou

图4-4　周天子与诸侯等级制的重要标识——鼎与簋
（河南博物院藏，河南新郑出土，春秋时期）

Fig. 4-4　Ding and Gui, important indicators of hierarchy of the Zhou Dynasty (collected in Henan Museum, unearthed in Xinzheng of Henan Province, Spring and Autumn Period)

问代表周王室权力正统的九鼎之大小轻重，王孙满巧妙地回复说国家的兴盛在于施行德义，不在鼎之大小，此为"问鼎中原"典故之由来。楚庄王问鼎中原之行为，体现了东周后期礼崩乐坏的混乱局面，但其觊觎取代之心理，亦反映出楚国对周代礼乐文明秩序的向往和认可（图4-4）。

（2）四面楚歌：西汉的建立与秦、楚文化的融合

秦灭六国，在中国首次实现了书同文、车同轨的大一统局面，把黄河流域关中地区的秦国制度文化强制在全国推行，抗争反弹最剧烈的就是处于长江、淮河流域的楚国地区。秦末天下大乱，首先起义的陈胜、吴广，以及后来灭秦而逐鹿天下的西楚霸王项羽、汉王刘邦，都肇发于楚国旧疆域之内。项羽最终被刘邦的汉军围困垓下，夜里听闻四面楚歌骤起，以为刘邦已经把楚国旧地全部占领，感慨大势已去，无力回天。

Dynasty, paid tribute now and then, and fused with the nationalities of the South, and all this made the Chu culture full of vigor and vitality, and indirectly made the Yellow River civilization of the Central Plains spread incessantly to the Yangtze River reaches. In 607 BC, the King Zhuang of Chu waged war northward to the periphery of Luoyang, the capital of Eastern Zhou, and held a military parade ceremony there. The King Ding of Zhou sent his representative Wangsun Man to express their good wishes and present gifts, whereas the King Zhuang of Chu directly asked about the weight of the nine Dings, which were symbols of the rightful power of the Zhou Dynasty. Wangsun Man skillfully answered that the prosperity of a state lied in the implementation of virtue and faith, not in the weight of the Dings. This is the story of "asking about the weight of tripod Ding in the Central Plains." The inquiry about the weight of Ding by the King Zhuang of Chu reflected the collapse of the rites of the Eastern Zhou Dynasty, but it also showed that the State of Chu longed for and identified with the rite-music civilization (Fig. 4-4).

(2) Songs of Chu on All Sides: Establishment of the Western Han Dynasty and Fusion of Qin and Chu Cultures

After Qin annihilated the other six states, China achieved for the first time the same writing and the same carriage modes and implemented by force around the whole country the Qin culture and system of the Central Shaanxi Plain of the Yellow River reaches. This incurred strong opposition, and the most violent opposition took place in the scope of the State of Chu, which was situated in the reaches of the Yangtze River and the Huaihe River. At the end of the Qin Empire, uprisings frequently took place. The pioneering Chen Sheng and Wu Guang, Xiang Yu who ended the Qin Empire, and Liu Bang as King of Han, all developed in the former territory of the State of Chu. Xiang Yu was eventually surrounded by the Han military troops at Gaixia. When he at night heard the songs of Chu on all sides, and thought that Liu Bang had completely occupied all the territory of the former Chu, he committed suicide.

After this, Liu Bang unified China, and made Chang'an the capital which was near the Weihe River and a new dynasty called Western Han was established (Fig. 4-5). The Han Dynasty continued to adopt the political system of Qin, and to a great extent continued the Qin's bureaucracy and legal thought, but

此后刘邦统一中国,定都渭水流域之长安,建立西汉王朝(图4-5)。在政治制度上汉承秦制,很大程度上延续了秦代的官僚体系和法治思想,但亦吸取秦亡的教训,在治国思想和文化上亦融合了楚制和楚文化,形成了长期稳定的社会局面。代表黄河流域文化的北方秦制,与代表长江、淮河流域文化的南方楚制,经过激烈对立和错综复杂的融合之后,在汉代以后逐渐形成一种崭新的黄河文明,并以更为有效的辐射力度向南方扩散传播。

图4-5　汉高祖刘邦像

Fig. 4-5　Portrait of Liu Bang, the first emperor of the Han Dynasty

(3)南定百越:黄河文化向珠江流域的移植

公元前219年,秦始皇派遣50万大军平定岭南百越之地,并长期驻扎屯守,以南海郡番禺(今广州)为政治、军事中心控制珠江流域。秦亡后,旧将赵佗割据岭南自立,建立南越国。赵佗原为恒山郡真定县人(今河北正定县)(图4-6),其在岭南实施汉越融合的政策,鼓励汉族军士和当地妇女通婚,并把黄河流域先进的生产技术和制度文明推广实施。汉代建立后,赵佗向汉纳贡称臣,开展互市贸易,造就了岭南地区安定和睦的稳定形势。汉武帝时期,灭南越国,在岭南地区设置郡

it also drew a lesson from the fall of Qin. It incorporated the Chu system and culture of ruling a country, and formed a long and stable social atmosphere. The Northern Qin system standing for the Yellow River culture and the Southern Chu system standing for the Yangtze and Huaihe culture, after fierce opposition and complicated fusion, gradually developed after the Han Dynasty into a fresh new Yellow River civilization, and disseminated and spread to the South with more efficient influential power.

(3) Pacifying Hundred-Yue: Migration of the Yellow River Culture to the Zhujiang Basin

In 219 BC, the First Emperor of the Qin Dynasty sent five hundred thousand troops to pacify the Hundred-Yue areas, and long stayed and camped there, controlling the reaches of Zhujiang with Panyu (today's Guangzhou) of Southsea County as its political and military center. After the fall of the Qin Dynasty, the former Qin general Zhao Tuo occupied Lingnan and claimed king himself, and established the State of Nan-Yue. Zhao Tuo was born in Zhending (today's Zhengding County, Hebei Province) (Fig. 4-6), implemented in Lingnan the Han-Yue fusion policy, encouraged the intermarriage between the generals and soldiers of the Han nationality and the local women, and popularized the advanced productive skills and system civilization of the Yellow River Basin. After the Han Dynasty was founded, Zhao Tuo paid tribute to Han, promoted trade with each other, and created a stable and friendly state of affairs. In the period of the Emperor Wu of Han, the State of Nan-Yue was destroyed, and it was ruled directly by the central government through the newly established prefectures and counties.

Thereafter, the technologies of cultivation, iron smelting, city building were transmitted to the Zhujiang Basin, and the characters, laws, political systems were subsequently promulgated, which accelerated the development of productive force and the spread of the Central Plains culture in the Lingnan areas, promoting the nationality fusion and social advancement in the Zhujiang Basin.

县，纳入中央直接统治版图。

自此，黄河流域的农耕、冶铁、筑城技术传入珠江流域，文字、法律、政治制度亦相继推广，加快了岭南地区生产力的发展和中原文化的传播，促进了珠江流域的民族融合和社会进步。

图4-6　赵佗故里家族墓墓碑（河北省正定县）

Fig. 4-6　Zhao Tuo family tomb stele, Zhengding County of Hebei Province

（4）涓滴渗透：黄河文化在红河流域的传播

汉武帝平定岭南后，在今越南中、北部的红河流域设置交趾、日南、九真三郡（图4-7），直至唐代设置安南都护府，红河流域作为中国的最南边疆长达千年。中央派遣郡县官吏进行治理，驻扎军队以威慑镇守，并在当地推行儒家文化教育，推选优秀的文化士人至中原学习任职。尤其是中央政府任命的地方官员，大都受过良好的儒家教育，具有强烈的将中华文明在帝国边疆传播的使命感，大大促进了中原礼制文明在越北地区的传播。如《后汉书》记载东汉时期交趾太守锡光、九真太守任延，

河源之畔 摄影/陈维达
The bank of the Yellow River headwater (photo by Chen Weida)

"教其耕稼，制为冠履，初设媒娉，始知姻娶，建立学校，导之礼义"，促使当地由"人如禽兽，长幼无别"的原始状态迈入儒家礼法文明体制之中，百姓感激敬畏，生子后乃至以其姓冠名。

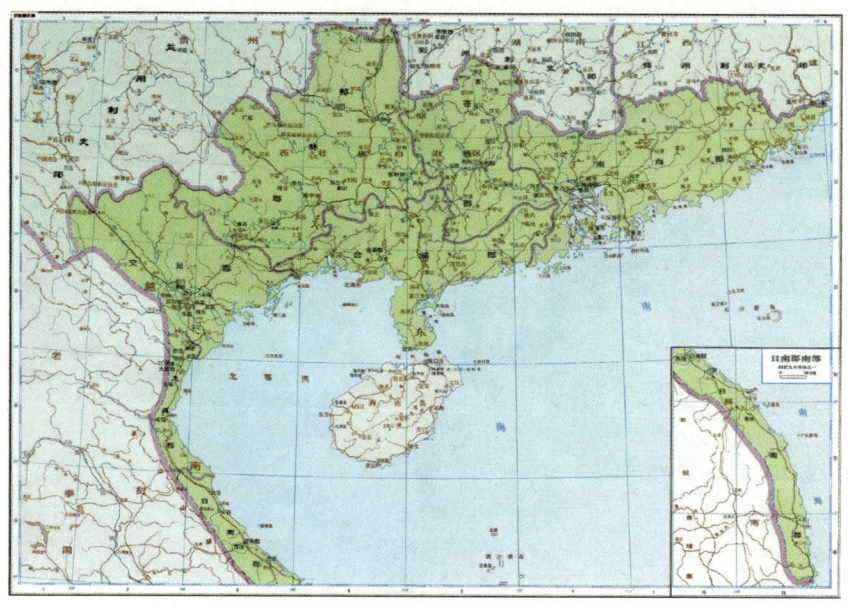

图4-7　西汉交阯刺史部示意图
谭其骧：《中国历史地图集》，中国地图出版社，1982年版
Fig. 4-7　Sketch map of Jiaozhi in the Western Han Dynasty
Tan Qixiang: *Chinese Historical Atlas*, Chinese Cartographic Publishing House, 1982 edition

经过长期郡县治理的涓滴渗透，以黄河文化为核心的中原文明已经深深地融入安南地区本土意识形态当中，加上更多汉族移民定居此地，其与中原地区的文化交流愈来愈密切，产生了一批深受汉文化影响素质优异的上层知识阶层，如唐德宗时期的爱州士人姜公辅，官至宰相。这对后世越南历史的发展走向产生了不可逆转的深刻影响。

(4) Dripping and Infiltration: Spread of the Yellow River Culture in the Honghe Basin

After the Emperor Wu of Han pacified Lingnan, prefectures of Jiaozhi, Rinan and Jiuzhen (Fig. 4-7) were established in today's central and northern Vietnam's Honghe Basin. Until An'nan Duhufu was set in the Tang Dynasty, the Honghe Basin had been the southern frontier of China for a thousand years. The central government sent officials at the prefecture and county levels to govern, sent military troops to settle there and keep peace, and carried out there Confucian cultural education, and recommended and selected elite cultural scholars to study and take office in the Central China. Especially the local officials appointed by the central government mostly received excellent Confucian education, and they had strong sense of mission to spread the Chinese civilization in the frontiers of the empire, which contributed greatly to the popularity of the Central Plains' civilization of rites in the areas that became today's northern Vietnam. According to *History of the Later Han Dynasty*, in the Eastern Han Dynasty, Xi Guang, governor of Jiaozhi, and Ren Yan, governor of Jiuzhen, "taught the local people how to cultivate and make hats and shoes, taught them how to make engagements and let them know for the first time about marriage, helped them to set up schools, and instructed them with rites and faith," which encouraged the people to develop from the primitive state of "men being like beasts, no difference between young and old" to grasping the Confucian system of rites and law, and the local people appreciated the efforts very much, and took the surnames of them for their children.

After long-term governance of the prefectures and counties, the Central Plains civilization with the Yellow River civilization as its core was deeply integrated into the local ideology of An'nan area. In addition, more people of Han nationality migrated here, and the cultural intercourse with the Central Plains became more and more close, and a number of excellent men of letters of upper class who were deeply influenced by the Han culture appeared, a good example being Jiang Gongfu who was a celebrity of Aizhou during the reign of Emperor Dezong of Tang and was ever promoted as prime minister.

二、兼容并蓄：异质文化之借鉴吸收

黄河文化作为一种农业文明，天然具有敦厚深沉、兼容并蓄的保守主义包容性格，较少具有扩张侵略性。另外，儒家文明具有早熟特质，自秦汉以来即把神权从政权中剥离，具有鲜明的世俗官僚主义、现实理性色彩。与历史上欧洲、中亚基督教、伊斯兰教文明的一元化、排他性相比，儒家文明对异质文明成果往往采取相对开放宽容的态度，更善于吸收借鉴，这对黄河文化的不断壮大发展产生了积极有益的深远影响。

1. 丝路先驱：张骞出使西域

张骞（公元前164年—前114年），西汉著名的外交家，今陕西城固县人（图4-8），在汉武帝时以两次出使西域、开辟丝绸之路而闻名于世，受封为博望侯。司马迁所撰《史记》盛赞张骞之壮举为"凿空"，意即首次打通了河西走廊至西域之通道。自此以后，中国人的世界地理

图4-8 陕西城固县张骞纪念馆2019年祭祀张骞典礼
Fig. 4-8　2019 ceremonial rite in honor of Zhang Qian in Chenggu County of Shaanxi Province

II. Inclusiveness and Incorporation: Absorption of Heterogeneous Culture

As an agricultural culture, the Yellow River culture is deep and conservatively inclusive by nature and shows rather little aggression. In addition, the Confucian civilization has characteristic of prematurity. The divine power has been removed from the political power since the Qin and Han dynasties, and a remarkable color of secular bureaucracy and realistic rationality can be easily discerned. Compared with the exclusiveness of European Christian and Central Asian Islamic civilizations, the Confucian civilization often adopted a relatively open and tolerant attitude towards the outcomes from the outside civilizations, which exerted a prolong and far-reaching influence on the continuous growth of the Yellow River culture.

1. Trailblazer of the Silk Road: Zhang Qian Was Sent on a Diplomatic Mission to the Western Regions

Zhang Qian (164 BC-114 BC), the famous diplomat in the Western Han Dynasty, was born in the County of Chenggu, Shaanxi Province (Fig. 4-8). He was sent during the reign of the Emperor Wu of Han twice as an ambassador to the Western Regions, opened up the Silk Road and was thus well-known to the world, and was entitled the count of Bowang. *The Historical Records* written by Sima Qian praised Zhang Qian as a trailblazer because of his feats, which meant that it was he who for the first time opened up the route that linked the Hexi Corridor with the Western Regions. Since then, the horizon of knowledge about the world geography of the Chinese was greatly broadened, and the ambassadors between the Han Dynasty and the Western Regions and the Central Asian states were incessantly on the movement in between, and the busy and smooth commercial communication on this road greatly promoted the communication between the East and the West civilizations. The agricultural irrigation, iron smelting, and textile technologies of the Central Plains Yellow River civilization were transmitted to the West, such new produce as pomegranate, flax, alfalfa and grape were introduced into China, and the cultural and art achievements from the

认知范围得到很大的拓展，汉代与西域、中亚诸国的使者络绎不绝，商路畅通，极大地促进了东西方文明的交流。中原黄河文明的农业灌溉、冶铁、纺织技术西传，而西域的石榴、胡麻、苜蓿、葡萄等新的作物品种被引入中国，来自中亚、南亚的音乐、雕塑、绘画、宗教等文化艺术成就亦逐渐传入，被黄河文化所接纳吸收。

2. 佛教东传：法显西行求法

佛教起源自印度，在东汉末年传入中国，相对注重现实理性的汉代儒家经学思想，其在阐释天地万物产生发展根本依据的本体论及对人生意义的终极关怀方面，教义更为缜密深刻，亦更符合下层百姓的精神依靠需求，渐渐笃信者众。至魏晋南北朝时期佛教发展鼎盛，对上、下层社会意识形态都产生了深刻的影响。而佛教作为外来文化，对以儒家思想为代表的黄河文化产生了巨大的冲击，并引发了激烈的碰撞交锋。佛教如何与中国文化有机融合，佛教教义的阐述如何实现本土化以贴合中国实际，是当时中国佛教信徒亟待解决的重大问题。而开启佛教中国化进程的关键人物，首推东晋高僧法显。

法显（公元334年—420年）（图4-9），今山西临汾人，是中国首位成功抵达天竺取经求法的高僧。公元399年，65岁高龄的法显从长安出发，经历西域30余国，至天竺寻求佛教经籍，足迹遍及南印度各国，从狮子国（今斯里兰卡）经南洋海路归国。归国后翻译了多部佛教经典，为解决国内佛学教义分歧做出了巨大的贡献。其所著《佛国记》保留了大量古代印度及斯里兰卡文化、历史资料，弥足珍贵。法显西行求法，标志着佛教在中国传播方式的重大转变，由之前依靠西域胡僧翻译传播，转变为中国人主动接受适应并积极与中国本土文化融合。

Middle and Southern Asia such as music, sculpture, painting and religion were also brought into China and were absorbed by the Yellow River culture.

2. Eastern Transmission of Buddhism: Fa-hsien Seeking for Buddha Dharma after a Western Journey

The Buddhism originated in India, and was transmitted into China at the end of the Eastern Han Dynasty. Compared with the realistic and rationalistic Confucian thought of the Han Dynasty, Buddhist teachings were more profound and systematic, and could be in more compliance with the spiritual reliance needs of the lower class inhabitants, so it gradually attracted a great number of believers. By the Wei, Jin, Northern and Southern dynasties, the development of Buddhism reached the apex, and exerted a deep influence on the ideology of the lower and the upper society. Buddhism as a foreign culture brought a huge impact on the Yellow River culture with Confucian thought as its representative, and stirred up fierce collision and engagement. How Buddhism could organically be integrated with the Chinese culture, and how the interpretations of the Buddhist teachings could be localized to adapt to the actuality of China were important problems to be solved by the Chinese believers of contemporary China. In the process of making Buddhism adapt to China, the most prominent and key historical figure was Fa-hsien, an eminent monk of the Eastern Jin Dynasty.

Fa-hsien (334-420 AD) (Fig. 4-9) was born in today's Linfen, Shanxi Province, and was the first Chinese monk to fetch the Buddhist scriptures and seek dharma after arriving in India. In 399 AD, Fa-hsien left Chang'an at the age of 65. After crossing more than thirty countries, he reached India to seek for the Buddhist scriptures and travelled around the South India, and returned to China from today's Sri Lanka through the sea route of the South Ocean. After returning back he translated many Buddhist scriptures, and made great contributions to solving the ambiguities of the Buddhist teachings in China. *The Record of Buddhist Countries* written by Fa-hsien preserved many cultural and historical materials of ancient India and Sri Lanka and was very precious. The fact that Fa-hsien went to the West to seek Dharma symbolized a major change of the way the Buddhism spread in China: from the former passive way of relying on the monks from the West to translate scriptures and spread Buddhism to an active way of

图4-9 法显像

Fig. 4-9 Portrait of Fa-hsien

3. 文化大使：玄奘天竺取经

玄奘（公元602年—664年）（图4-10），唐代著名高僧、佛教翻译家，今河南偃师县人，被后世尊称为"三藏法师"。其历尽万险至天竺舍身求法的故事广为流传，所撰《大唐西域记》被视为研究古代印度历史的宝库，其本人被誉为中印文化交流的杰出使者。

佛教发展至唐代，南北教义学说分歧依然，至玄奘求取大量佛教原典，苦心翻译，博采众长，开宗立派，成为继承印度正统佛教学说的集大成者，也极大地促进了佛教中国化的进程。

唐代以后，中国佛教发展出很多流派，主要有法性宗、法相宗、天台宗、华严宗、净土宗、密宗、禅宗、律宗八大宗派。其中禅宗的中国本土化最为成功，成为黄河流域宗教文化的典型代表，流传最为广泛，影响逐渐扩大到整个东亚地区。

accepting, adapting to the Chinese local culture and fusing with each other.

3. Cultural Ambassador: Hsuan-tsang Seeking Buddhist Truths in India

Hsuan-tsang (602-664 AD) (Fig. 4-10) was a famous monk and translator of Buddhist scriptures in the Tang Dynasty. He was born in today's Yanshi, Henan Province, and was called respectfully as "Tripitaka Dharma Master" by later generations. The story of his seeking Buddhist truths in India after experiencing dangers and difficulties of all kinds was well-known, and his *Tang- Dynasty Records of the Western Regions* (*Datang Xiyu Ji*) was considered to be a treasure for the study of ancient Indian history, and Hsuan-tsang himself was praised as an outstanding ambassador of Sino-Indian cultural communication.

When Buddhism developed till the Tang Dynasty, there still existed difference between the northern and the southern Buddhist teachings. Hsuan-tsang fetched a huge number of original scriptures and translated them into Chinese. Chinese Buddhism became a new denomination that inherited the Indian orthodox Buddhism and his effort greatly promoted the adaptation of Buddhism in China.

Since the Tang Dynasty, China's Buddhism developed into many branches, mainly including the Dharma Pakati School, the Dharma Lakkhana School, the Tiantai School, the Avatamsaka School, the Zen School, the Sukhavativyuha School, the Vinaya School, and the Mantrayana School. The Zen School was the most successful in the localization in China, and became the typical representative of religious culture in the Yellow River Basin, and its influence was the most widespread, covering the whole East Asia.

图4-10　玄奘负笈西行图
Fig. 4-10　Hsuan-tsang on a Western Journey

4. 佛道交融：禅宗的形成

禅宗相传由南北朝时期印度高僧菩提达摩所创，在唐代发展鼎盛，尊登封少林寺为祖庭肇发地。后在中国南北各地开枝散叶，形成"五家七宗"之派别，门庭繁茂，渐成中国佛教思想的主流（图4-11）。又东传朝鲜、日本，南传越南等地，朝鲜"九山禅门"、日本"禅宗二十四流"、越南"竹林禅宗"皆为其外传支系。

禅宗最显著的特点即吸收中国传统道家"心性自然"的哲学观点，把道家老庄思想中的自然主义、自由观念融入佛教教义中，使烦琐的佛教教义简单化，讲究"顿悟成佛"，主张"人人皆有佛性"，更易被普通民众所接受，也彻底实现了佛教的中国化过程。

禅宗的形成，可以视为中国本土黄河文化对外来文化的积极改造和吸收，它没有囫囵吞枣式地照搬印度佛学，而是通过富有实践精神的积极创新，使得佛教在很大程度上成了一种中国宗教，并焕发出新的生机活力。

4. Fusion of Buddhism and Taoism: Formation of Zen Buddhism

The Zen Buddhism was said to be created by the Indian eminent monk Bodhidharma, and reached its zenith in the Tang Dynasty. Zen Buddhism regarded Shaolin Temple in Dengfeng as its inception place. It then developed into "five sects and seven denominations" in the north and south of China, and gradually became the mainstream of Buddhist thought in China (Fig. 4-11). It was then transmitted to Korea, Japan, Vietnam and had various branches in these countries respectively.

The most remarkable characteristic of Zen Buddhism was that it absorbed the traditional Chinese Taoist philosophical viewpoint of "natural disposition," integrated the naturalism and the ideal of freedom from the thought of Lao Tseu and Chuang Tzu into the Buddhist teachings, and made the complicated teachings more simple. It advocated "sudden revelation to gain Buddhist truth," and proposed that "all believers have Buddhist nature," which was more easily accepted by the common people, and completely realized its Chinese localization.

The formation of Zen Buddhism can be considered to be an active transformation and absorption of froeign culture by the Chinese native Yellow River culture. It did not copy completely the Indian Buddhism, but actively created with practical spirit and made Buddhism to a great extent a Chinese religion, and boomed with new vigor.

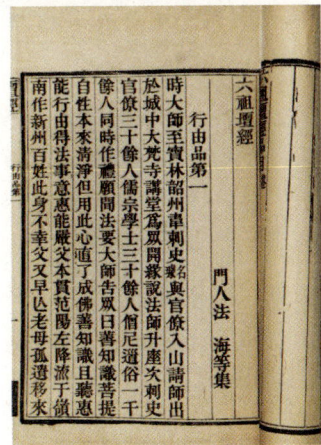

图4-11 禅宗经典《六祖坛经》

Fig. 4-11 Zen Buddhist Classic—*Tan Scriptures*

5. 以禅入儒：理学思想的兴起

理学又称"道学"，主要探讨万事万物的本源——义理之学，形成于宋代，实现了对传统汉唐儒学的跨越和革新，占据了后世儒家意识形态的主流，近代西方人称其为"新儒家"（Neo-Confucianism）。其中起源于河洛地区的"洛学"，以"二程先生"（程颢、程颐）学说为代表（图4-12），为理学思想奠定了重要的基础。

图4-12　河南嵩县程村二程故里建筑

Fig. 4-12　Building of former residence of Cheng Hao and Cheng Yi in Chengcun Village, Song County, Henan Province

宋代理学的形成，与唐代以来士大夫禅学的兴起有着极为重要的关联。禅宗在中国化的过程中，将其实现生命意义超越的通透智慧，都融化到儒家哲学对人生的肯定和厚重的伦理人情之中，形成了中国化佛禅与儒学相互交融的精神理路。富有思辨深度的禅宗哲学外在刺激促进了儒学思想本身的自省，使其获得了内在创发性的突破，吸纳了佛教的思辨模式、理论形态并重新焕发活力。

5. Incorporating Zen into Confucianism: Rise of the Thought of Neo-Confucianism

The Neo-Confucianism was also called "scholarship of Dao," mainly dealing with the origin of all things—scholarship of meaning and rationality, and it was formed in the Song Dynasty. It realized the great leap and innovation beyond the traditional Han-Tang Confucianism, and occupied the mainstream among the Confucian ideologies of later generations. The "scholarship of Luo" that originated in the Yellow River-Luoyang areas had Cheng Hao and Cheng Yi as its representatives (Fig. 4-12), and laid important foundation for the thought of Neo-Confucianism.

The formation of Song Dynasty's Neo-Confucianism had extremely important connection with the rise of the scholars' Zen Buddhism since the Tang Dynasty. In the development of the Zen Buddhism, it combined the great wisdom of realizing the transcendence of meaning of life with the strong ethics and reaffirmation of life of the Confucian philosophy, and shaped into a spiritual context of fusing the Buddhism, Zen and Confucianism characteristics of Chinese mode. Confucianism in turn realized its own breakthrough as a result of the outside stimulation of the Zen Buddhist philosophy with a high level of critical thinking.

The Neo-Confucianism of the Song Dynasty reannotated the Confucian classics with the Buddhist theory, and solved the long-existed problem of want of metaphysical ontology for the Confucianism and made great compensation in the individual settlement, philosophical thinking and mind and body fostering. The Neo-Confucianist theorists placed the traditional Confucianist morality and human nature beneath the roots of the Tao of Heaven, and made Chinese cultural philosophy become more rationalist, and took on a more splendid look in its spiritual aspect.

宋代理学采用佛教精粹义理重新注疏儒家经典，吸纳佛禅严密的哲理和精密的修行方法，解决长期以来儒家在形上本体的认识和具体工夫方面的缺漏问题，很大程度上弥补了儒学在个体安顿、哲学思辨、身心修养方面的不足。理学家将传统儒家的道德和人性置于天道的根源之下，使中国文化哲学更加趋于理性化、注重自觉性，呈现出更为宏大的精神境界。

6. 融会中西：犍陀罗艺术的传播

犍陀罗艺术，1—5 世纪流行于南亚次大陆西北部贵霜帝国的佛教艺术，兼具印度和希腊风格。佛教传入中国，对魏晋南北朝、隋唐时期的艺术产生了巨大的影响，并逐渐形成了具有中国特色的艺术风格。

犍陀罗艺术最典型的代表是佛像雕刻，同佛寺建筑、壁画共同组成一个完整的视觉整体。北魏时期大同云冈石窟还是典型的犍陀罗艺术风格，但唐代洛阳龙门石窟佛像塑造风格已经被中国文化所融合改造，面

图4-13　河南洛阳龙门石窟卢舍那大佛

Fig. 4-13　Vairocana Buddha Statue, Longmen Grottos in Luoyang City, Henan Province

6. Fusion of China and the West: Spread of the Gandhara Art

The Gandhara art was a kind of Buddhist arts that was popular between the first and fifth century in the Kushan Empire which was situated in the northwest of the South Asian Subcontinent, and it had both the Indian and Greek features. With the introduction into China of the Buddhism, it exerted a huge influence on the art of the Wei and Jin, and Sui and Tang dynasties, and gradually a new style of art with characteristics of China was shaped.

The most typical representative of the Gandhara art was the Buddhist statue carving, which constituted a complete visual whole together with the Buddhist temple architectures and the mural paintings. Yungang Grottos of the Northern Wei Dynasty had still the typical style of the Gandhara art, but the Buddhist statues' style of Longmen Grottos of the Tang Dynasty was reshaped by and merged with the Chinese culture, and the facial profiles and the body features demonstrated more characteristics of the oriental nationality (Fig. 4-13), and a very conspicuous characteristic of the Tang Dynasty was formed. Furthermore, the Gandhara style Buddhist pagoda also combined with the aboriginal Chinese pavilions to form a kind of frequently seen multi-layer pagoda.

A large number of Chinese style Gandhara Buddha statues and Buddhist pagodas that have been preserved till now are witnessing the brilliance of the fusion between the oriental and occidental cultures. After the Gandhara art disappeared in the Middle and West Asia, it was absorbed and preserved by the Central Plains culture of the Yellow River Basin, gradually developed into a peculiar and distinctive symbol of Huaxia civilization, and became a treasure of East Asia after it was transmitted to Korea and Japan.

7. Prosperity Ethos: Foreign Arts of the Tang Dynasty

The Tang Dynasty was one era having the most plentiful nationalities and the most open and tolerant atmosphere to various ideas in the history of China. Appreciation and acceptance of foreign arts were very popular at that time, including all classes from the courtiers and aristocracy to the urban inhabitants, and an era ethos full of prosperity and confidence emerged. Chang'an and Luoyang as two capitals of the Tang Dynasty attracted foreign officials and merchants of too many countries, and the peculiar clothing, music and dance

目轮廓、体态特征更富有东方民族气质（图 4-13），形成了鲜明的唐代特征。另外，犍陀罗式佛塔也和中国固有的楼阁形式结合，形成常见的多层宝塔。

众多保存至今的中国式犍陀罗佛像与寺塔，见证着东西方文化相融合后的辉煌，在犍陀罗艺术在中西亚地区衰亡消失后，被黄河流域中原文化所吸纳保存，逐渐成为独具特色的华夏文明标识，并东传至朝鲜、日本，成为东亚艺术之瑰宝。

7. 盛世气象：唐代域外艺术

唐代为中国历史上民族构成最为丰富、思想最为包容开放之时代。欣赏、接纳域外艺术的社会风气盛行一时，从宫廷贵族蔓延至城市居民的各个阶层，呈现出富强自信的盛世气象。唐代两京长安、洛阳为万国来朝之所，外商辐辏聚集之地，来自西域的奇装异服（图 4-14）、炫人耳目的胡乐胡舞，无不被模仿流传，唐代诗人王建有"洛阳家家学胡乐"之语。胡旋、飞天舞激扬优美的姿态，在敦煌壁画鲜艳的色彩中得到完美的呈现；龟兹曲项琵琶珠落玉盘般的清脆之音，至今成为中国传统音乐的绝美华章；西域晕染凸凹的立体画法，成就了吴道子"吴代当风"的生动画风，达到盛唐绘画艺术的巅峰。

源远流长的黄河文化，海纳百川，有容乃大，通过不断借鉴、吸收域外文明优秀成分，逐步丰富壮大并适应时代的发展要求，成为中华民族不朽的精神象征和力量源泉。

from the Western Regions were all imitated and spread by the local people. The gesture and posture of the Huxuan dance and Feitian dance were perfectly represented in the splendid colors of the Dunhuang mural paintings. The melody out of the crooked Pipa of Qiuci is now still a wonderful representative of traditional Chinese music. The cubism painting approach of the Western Regions contributed to the development of the lively painting style of Wu Daozi, which reached the zenith of the painting art of the flourishing Tang Dynasty.

The Yellow River culture that is long standing and well established is tolerant and all-embracing, so it can continuously absorb and draw on the positive experience of foreign civilizations and gradually grow and develop to adapt itself to the demands of the new era, and becomes the ever-lasting spiritual symbol and power source of the Chinese nationality.

图4-14　唐章怀太子墓壁画中的外国使者

Fig. 4-14　Foreign diplomats depicted in the tomb of Prince Zhanghuai of the Tang Dynasty

三、光芒四射：黄河文化的域外影响

黄河流域孕育出东亚地区最早的国家形态和先进的政治制度，黄河文化是中华文化的代表和象征。在历史进程中，成熟包容、同化能力强的黄河文化犹如核心热源般光芒四射，不断辐射影响周边地区和国家，在东亚形成朝鲜、越南、日本、琉球汉字文化圈，在东南亚地区形成以中国为中心的朝贡体系，乃至对中亚、欧洲等域外国家的经济、文化发展产生过持续而积极的影响。

1. 东国中华：朝鲜

朝鲜历史上与中国渊源最深，箕子朝鲜与卫满朝鲜传说都是由中国贵族移民所建立，汉代曾在朝鲜半岛北部设立郡县，持续引入黄河流域先进的生产技术和政治文明。新罗与唐朝关系最为密切，积极输入中原文化，遣唐使崔致远在唐朝科举及第，在朝鲜历史上享有崇高声誉，被尊为"百世之师"。其后的高丽和李氏朝鲜王朝均以中国为宗主国，奉儒家文化为圭臬（图4-15），实施科举取士，移植华夏政治制度；尤其是李氏朝鲜时期，极力推崇宋明理学，以"小中华"正统地位自居。

2. 汉唐衣冠：越南

今越南中北部地区，在汉、唐时期受中国郡县统治长达千年，汉曰交趾，唐曰安南都护府。中原黄河文化通过地方长官的推行，以及内地移民持续不绝的渗透，对当地政治、文化趋向起到了决定性的影响。至北宋初期始独立建国，但一直作为藩臣对中国历代王朝定期朝贡，北宋赐国号安南，至清代始改越南。在文化上一直以汉字为官方正统文字（图4-16），政治上模仿唐、宋制度，开科举、设职官。14世纪末胡朝太上皇胡季犛曾作诗言："欲问安南事，安南风俗淳。衣冠唐制度，礼乐

III. Brilliance and Glory: Influence of the Yellow River Culture on Foreign Countries

The Yellow River Basin has fostered the earliest state form and advanced political system of the East Asian regions, and the Yellow River culture is the symbol and representative of Chinese culture. In the advancement of history, like source of radiation, the Yellow River culture incessantly influenced the surrounding regions and countries, helped to form the cultural circle of Chinese characters in such East Asian countries as Korea, Vietnam, Japan and the Ryukyu Islands, and a tribute system with China being the center was formed in the Southeast Asian regions, and it even exerted continuous and positive influence on the economy and culture of the countries in the Central Asia and Europe.

1. East to China: Korea

Korea shared the most profound historical relationship with China, and such legends as Jizi Korea and Weiman Korea asserted that both of them were established by the migrant Chinese nobility. In the Han Dynasty, prefectures and

图4-15　古代朝鲜国子监——成均馆大成殿

Fig. 4-15　Sungkyunkwan, ancient Korean Imperial College

汉君臣。"15世纪黎朝建立后,确立儒家思想为治国根本,全面输入明代制度文化,以中华文献之邦傲视周边,不断向南方开疆拓土。至越南阮朝时期把儒家文化渐次推广至湄公河流域。

图4-16　15世纪越南官修正史《大越史记全书》

Fig. 4-16　*The Complete History of Great Vietnam*, official history complied in the 15th century

3. 海外唐风：日本

日本与中国隔海相望,与朝鲜、越南历史不同,未受过中国封建王朝的直接统治,宗藩关系亦不固定。但中国文化对日本的影响却同样深远,主要体现在日本对以黄河文化为核心的唐代文化的主动学习。7世纪中叶,"大化革新"掀起了日本社会全面唐化的高潮,日本派出大量遣唐使,积极学习大陆文明,建立律令制国家。日本在封建社会时期持续关注并引入中华文明成果,从汉字到唐诗,从音乐到绘画,从儒家典籍到禅宗思想,从服饰起居到建筑样式,在日本都带有鲜明的唐风遗韵(图4-17)。

counties were established in the north of the Korean Peninsula, and the advanced productive technology and political civilization were continuously introduced there. Silla had a close relationship with the Tang Dynasty, actively introduced the Central Plains culture, and the diplomat Cui Zhiyuan passed the imperial examination in the Tang Dynasty and enjoyed a high reputation in the history of Korea with the title of "master of a hundred generations." The subsequent Koryo and Choson dynasties both regarded China as suzerain and observed the Confucian culture closely. They also adopted the practice of selecting the officials through imperial examination and introduced the political system of China; and the Choson Dynasty in particular held Song-Ming Confucianism in extremely high esteem, and boasted itself as "little China."

2. Han-Tang Style Clothing: Vietnam

The central and northern regions of today's Vietnam were ruled as prefectures and counties for a thousand years in the dynasties of Han and Tang, and they were called Jiaozhi in the Han Dynasty and An'nan Duhufu in the Tang Dynasty. The Central Plains Yellow River culture, as a result of the implementation by the local administrators and the continuous immigration of the inland people, exerted a decisive influence on the trend of the local politics and culture. Vietnam gained independence from the start of the Northern Song Dynasty, but it always paid tribute to the successive dynasties of China as a vassal state. It was granted the name of State An'nan, and was renamed Vietnam from the Qing Dynasty. Vietnam adopted Chinese characters as the official orthodox written language, and in imitation of the political systems of the Tang and Song dynasties, it carried out the imperial examination and set up official posts of various kinds. At the end of the fourteenth century, the father of the contemporary emperor Hu Jimao ever wrote a poem in praise of the imitation of clothing of the Tang Dynasty and the adoption of rites and music of the Han Dynasty. After the establishment of the Li Dynasty in the fifteenth century, the Confucianism was established as the basic ideology of ruling the country, and the Ming Dynasty's system and culture were introduced comprehensively, and Li Dynasty boasted itself as being the country of possessing Chinese tradition, and expanded its territory southward. By the Ruan Dynasty, Vietnam had gradually made the Confucian culture popular along the

图4-17　日本奈良唐式建筑东大寺

Fig. 4-17　Todai Temple located in Nara, Japan: a building typical of the Tang Dynasty

4. 改变世界："四大发明"的西传

造纸术、印刷术、指南针、火药统称源自中国的"四大发明",据相关研究指出都起源自两汉、唐宋时期的黄河流域,是黄河文化物质成就的典型代表。马克思曾指出:"火药、指南针、印刷术——这是预告资产阶级社会到来的三大发明。火药把骑士阶层炸得粉碎,指南针打开了世界市场并建立了殖民地,而印刷术则变成了新教的工具(图4-18),总的来说变成了科学复兴的手段,变成对精神发展创造必要前提的最强大的杠杆",其评价可谓精辟公允。"四大发明"随着海上和陆上丝绸之路逐渐传播至中东、欧洲诸国,对世界文明的进步和近代欧洲文艺复兴、宗教革命、大航海时代的兴起起到了积极的推动作用,充分体现了黄河文化对世界历史进程的巨大影响。

reaches of the Mekong River.

3. Oversea Atmosphere of the Tang Dynasty: Japan

Japan is China's neighbor across a reach of sea. It was historically different from Korea and Vietnam since it had not been directly ruled by China's feudalist dynasties, and it did not recognize China as a suzerain for a long period of time. But China's culture still exerted a profound influence on Japan mainly in that Japan ever studied the Tang Dynasty's culture with the Yellow River culture as the core on its own. In the middle of the seventh century, Taika Reform made a complete imitation of the Tang Dynasty by the Japanese society, and a number of Kentoushi were sent to China to study actively the continental civilization and a country ruled by laws was established. Japan in its feudalist period incessantly paid attention to and introduced the Chinese culture, from Chinese characters to Tang poetry, from music to painting, from Confucian classics to Zen Buddhist ideas, from clothing and living styles to architectural style, all of which had conspicuous features of the Tang Dynasty (Fig. 4-17).

4. To Change the World: Spread of the Four Great Inventions to the West

Papermaking, printing, compass, gunpowder were called collectively the "Four Great Inventions of China." According to the research, they all originated from the Yellow River Basin areas in the Western and Eastern Han dynasties and the Tang and Song dynasties, and they were typical representatives of the Yellow River material culture. Marx pointed out, "Gunpowder, compass and printing were the three great inventions which ushered in bourgeois society. Gunpowder blew up the knightly class, compass opened the world market and founded the colonies, and printing was the instrument of Protestantism (Fig. 4-18) and the regeneration of science in general, and the most powerful lever for creating the intellectual prerequisites." And Marx made a fair comment. The four inventions were spread along the Maritime Silk Road and the Land Silk Road to the Middle East and the European countries, and played a positive role in the advancement of the world civilization, the European Renaissance, the religious revolution, and the rise of the Age of Discovery, which fully embodied the huge influence which the Yellow River culture exerted on the historical development of the world.

图4-18　15世纪德国活字印刷《古腾堡圣经》

Fig. 4-18　A movable-type printing classic—*Gutenberg Bible* in the 15th century Germany

5. 关注东方：17—19世纪欧洲汉学的兴起

13世纪意大利旅行家所撰《马可·波罗游记》在欧洲的广为流传，激起西方对文明富足的中国的热烈向往，成为西欧诸国探险家新航路开辟的重要驱动力。17世纪以后，大批耶稣会教士来华传教，他们积极学习汉语，并编纂汉字字典；研究中国儒家经典，从中挖掘便于传教的理论依据，最早开始了对"四书"的翻译研究；并着重介绍中国发达而先进的科举、文官制度，引发不少欧洲学者的赞赏关注，以黄河文明为代表的中国文化主要呈现正面的积极形象。19世纪以后，随着工业革命的开展和西欧海上霸权时代的开启，欧洲人开始以文明开化的轻视姿态审视中国文化，但同时由于拓展殖民地和文化掠夺的需要，亦涌现出一大批研究中国的东方学家，如法国三大汉学家沙畹、伯希和（图4-19）、谢阁兰即为典型代表。他们翻译了大量中国儒学、史学、文学典籍，并针对中国古代的政治、法律制度、文化宗教等方方面面开展研究，出版了一系列较有影响力的专著，在客观上亦推动了中国黄河文化在西方的传播。

5. Concern for the Orient: the Rise of European Sinology between the 17th and the 19th Century

The Travels of Marco Polo, written by Marco Polo, a 13th century Italian traveler, gained great popularity in Europe and ignited a great aspiration to the affluent and civilized China in the West, and constituted an important driving force for the Western European explorers to open the new lines of navigation. Since the 17th century, a large number of Jesuit missionaries came to China to preach the Christian teachings. They actively studied Chinese, and compiled Chinese dictionaries; they studied the Chinese classics in an attempt to find the theoretical foundations which facilitated their preaching and began for the first time the translation studies of the "Four Books" of China; they introduced with emphasis China's advanced imperial examination system and the civil service system, and attracted much attention and praise from many European scholars, and the Chinese culture with the Yellow River civilization being the representative was posed as a positive image. Since the 19th century, with the development of the Industrial Revolution and the initiation of the maritime hegemony of the Western Europe, the Europeans began to scrutinize Chinese culture condescendingly as if they were enlightened and civilized people. But as a result of the demands of expanding the colonies and conducting the cultural exploitation, a number of

图4-19 法国著名汉学家伯希和
Fig. 4-19 Paul Pelliot, a famous French sinologist

6. 现代转型：当代美国对黄河文明研究的拓展

二战以后，国际形势发生巨大变化，以美国为主导的世界政治、经济格局得以确立，随着中国地缘政治实力的不断提升，过去以欧洲为代表的传统汉学研究逐渐没落，而美国的中国学研究异军突起，呈现出新的时代特点，影响巨大。他们把研究的重点转至中国近现代的热点问题，并试图从中华黄河文明的历史进程中去探究这些问题形成的根源（图4-20）；尤其注重近现代中国政治发展、经济转型、社会治理、民生变化等方面的研究，观察角度细微，注重实证，并运用现代政治学、社会学理论进行深度的解释；亦十分关切以黄河文明为源头的中华帝国形成原因的探讨，从更宏观的角度去理解当代中国融入世界过程中，儒家文明与西方基督教文明的差异对抗性和冲击适应调整。这些改变了传统欧洲汉学静态单一的研究模式，即把中国古老的黄河文明视为精美优雅但缺乏生机的"博物馆藏品"，而忽视其发展变化和内在驱动力。美国汉学逐渐从传统走向现代，形成了当代美国中国学 (Chinese Studies)。

图4-20 美国当代著名汉学家比尔•波特（代表作《黄河之旅》等）
Fig. 4-20 Bill Porter, American contemporary famous sinologist (author of *A Journey along the Yellow River*)

Sinologists focusing on the study of China also rose to fame, with three French Sinologists Edouard Chavannes, Paul Pelliot (Fig. 4-19) and Victor Segalen as an example. They translated a large number of Chinese classics of Confucianism, history and literature, and conducted researches on ancient Chinese politics, legal system, culture and religion and so on, and published a series of influential books, which contributed objectively to the spread of Chinese Yellow River culture in the West.

6. Modern Transformation: Extension of Studies of the Yellow River Civilization in Contemporary America

The international situation experienced dramatic changes after the Second World War, and the political and economic world order dominated by America was established. With the continuous promotion of China's geopolitical power, the traditional Sinology studies represented by Europe gradually declined, and American studies of China rose rapidly and took on new features of the era and played a very important role. They shifted the focus of study to the hot issues of modern and contemporary China in an attempt to investigate the roots that shaped the problems from the historical advancement of Chinese Yellow River civilization (Fig. 4-20). They laid special emphasis on the studies of political development, economic transformation, social governance, social changes in modern and contemporary China, and they also showed much concern about the causes of the formation of the empire of China that had Yellow River civilization as its source. They understood from a more macroscopic perspective the heterogenous antagonism and adaptative adjustment between the Confucian civilization and the Western Christian civilization in the process of China's merging into the world. All this changed the static single research model of traditional European Sinology which considered Chinese ancient Yellow River civilization as an elegant "collection of museum" that lacked vigor, and overlooked the inner driving force of its development and change. American Sinology gradually developed from the traditional towards the modern into Chinese Studies in contemporary America.

长河落日 摄影/ 董保华
The sunset over the Yellow River (photo by Dong Baohua)

四、生生不息：黄河文化的再生与创新精神

　　元、明、清时期，由于黄河文化区政治、经济中心地位的丧失，以及理学思想僵化导致的社会禁锢，黄河文化失去了昔日吸收、消化异质文化的自信开放特色，逐渐走向衰落，文化模式保守定型，缺乏创新活力。面对1840年以来近代西方文化、工业技术的挑战冲击，明显缺乏主动同化、吸收西方先进文化的经济基础和民族自信，步履蹒跚，跌跌撞撞，被动地走向旧秩序解体的混乱局面。历史悠久、传承厚重的黄河文化面临千年以来未见之大变局，亟待新的突破和重生。古老的黄河文明，经过晚清时期洋务运动，民国时期对近代工业化、民主化体制追求探索的近代文明洗礼，历经将近100年步履蹒跚的曲折探索历程，终于在1949年中华人民共和国成立之后，迎来了全面恢复与快速发展的历史新局面。

1. 复苏：新中国成立以后黄河文化的发展

　　1949年中华人民共和国的成立，开启了中国迈向现代社会的新局面。通过对黄河流域综合治理的启动，社会秩序得到恢复，民生经济日新月异，教育文化建设有了长足的发展，为黄河文化的重生奠定了坚实的经济基础和人文底蕴。1978年中国共产党十一届三中全会以后，中国实施全面改革开放，开始了建设四个现代化的伟大进程，以沿海经济区为龙头，内地市场经济有了长足的发展，黄河流域延续几千年的传统农业文化发生了根本性的变革，工业化建设的步伐明显加快（图4-21），民众的思维方式、精神面貌有了翻天覆地的变化，为黄河文化的重生提供了关键的机遇。

IV. Everlasting Growth: Spirit of Regeneration and Creativity of the Yellow River Culture

In the dynasties of Yuan, Ming and Qing, the central regions of the Yellow River culture lost the place as the country's political and economic center, and at the same time the stereotyped Neo-Confucianism resulted in the social confinement, the Yellow River culture lost its confident and open characteristics that could absorb and digest heterogenous cultures, and gradually declined and the cultural mode became conservative and lacked creativity and vigor. When confronted with the challenges and shocks by the modern Western culture and industrial technology after 1840, it clearly lacked the economic foundation and national confidence that were needed to actively assimilate and integrate the advanced Western culture, and faltered towards the chaotic situation of disintegration of old order. The Yellow River culture faced an unprecedented transformation within a thousand years, and was in urgent need of new breakthrough and revival. The old Yellow River civilization, after the late Qing's Westernization Movement, and the striving for modern industrialization and system of democracy in the period of the Republic of China, eventually met with the new historical situation of overall rehabilitation and rapid development with the establishment of the People's Republic of China in 1949.

1. Revival: Development of the Yellow River Culture after the Founding of PRC

The founding of PRC in 1949 ushered in a new situation of China's advance into modern society. With the initiation of comprehensive treatment of the Yellow River Basin, the social order was restored, the people's life and economy experienced rapid growth, the education and culture gained great development, and all this laid a solid economic and humanistic foundation for the rebirth of the Yellow River culture. After the Third Plenary Session of the 11th CPC Central Committee, China implemented the policy of comprehensive reform and opening up and began the great enterprise of realizing the four modernizations. With the coastal economic areas being the pioneer, the inland market economy gained

图4-21 黄河中游大型水利枢纽工程——小浪底水力发电站

（河南省孟津县，2001年竣工）

Fig. 4-21 Xiaolangdi Hydraulic Power Station, large-scale hydraulic pivotal project in the middle reaches of the Yellow River (Mengjin County, Henan Province, completed in 2001)

2. 机遇：新时期黄河文化的重塑

迈入21世纪，随着改革开放政策的深化开展，中国的综合国力得到极大提升，国际地位和软实力大幅度提升。尤其是中国共产党十八大以来，习近平总书记发出的一带一路发展倡议（图4-22），展现了中国更加积极地融入世界格局、履行中国国际责任的决心，更加需要提倡中国的核心价值观和文化自信，推行文化"走出去"战略。而文化自信的根与魂，就是要弘扬以黄河文化为核心的中国传统文化，展示对传统思想价值体系的认同与尊崇，让黄河文化历久弥新，适应新时代发展的需求。这是时代赋予黄河文化重生、实现跨越式发展的一个重要战略机遇。

重塑黄河文化，不是恢复原来以旱地农业为主的农耕文化，而是要

dramatic development. The traditional agricultural culture that lasted for several thousand years in the Yellow River Basin experienced fundamental change, the pace of industrial construction accelerated (Fig. 4-21), the way of thinking and the mental state of the people were also greatly improved, and all this paved the way for the crucial opportunity of the rebirth of the Yellow River culture.

2. Opportunities: Reshaping of the Yellow River Culture in the New Era

After the entrance of the 21st century, with the deepening of the reform and opening-up policy, China's comprehensive national power has been drastically improved, and its international status and soft power have been greatly promoted. Especially since the 18th National Congress of the Communist Party of China, the Belt-and-Road Initiative (Fig. 4-22) sponsored by President Xi Jinping demonstrates the resolution of China to integrate into the world framework more actively and to perform the international responsibility of China, which is in more need of promoting the core values and cultural confidence of China and implementing the strategy of culture "going out." The root and soul of cultural confidence is to promote Chinese traditional culture with the Yellow River culture

图4-22 面向21世纪的中国 "一带一路" 倡议

Fig. 4-22 China's "Belt-and-Road" Initiative oriented towards the 21st century

以现代工业、农业和科学技术为基础,又创新发展古老黄河文化的精髓和有益成分,发展出有别于西方海洋文明而又立足本土、和谐共存、包容开放的新黄河文化。

3. 创新:继承黄河文化母体的变革精神

黄河文化具有自强不息、求变创新的母体精神。源自黄河流域的先秦文化具有鲜明的变革精神,《周易》即提出:"天地革而四时成""顺乎天而应乎人:革之时大矣哉!"认为变化是天地万物的根本规律,人应该顺应时代的变革。儒家原始典籍亦强调创新求变:"苟日新,日日新,又日新。"黄河流域在2000多年前能够形成发达领先的政治制度,与黄河文化强调适应时代,主动变革社会体制有很大的关系。先秦时期伟大改革家商鞅有言:"三代不同礼而王,五霸不同法而霸。"黄河文化母体具有强烈的现实关怀、求变图强的蓬勃朝气,是中华民族自强不息精神的重要源泉(图4-23)。当代黄河文化的新生,更加需要继承

图4-23　自强不息、激昂澎湃的中华民族精神象征:黄河壶口瀑布
Fig. 4-23　Hukou Waterfall of the Yellow River, symbol of unyielding spirit of Chinese nationality

as the core, to demonstrate the identification and respect of the traditional idea and value system, and to make the Yellow River culture anew and adapt to the demand of development in the new era. This is an important strategic opportunity posed by the era to empower the Yellow River culture and realize a great leap in development.

To reshape the Yellow River culture is not to restore the former agricultural culture which was mainly arid land agriculture, but, based on modern industrial, agricultural and scientific technology, and maintaining the positive elements of the old Yellow River culture, to develop a new Yellow River culture which is based on local tradition, harmonious coexistence, inclusiveness and openness but different from the Western maritime civilization.

3. Creativity: Inheritance of the Spirit of Reform of Parental Origin of the Yellow River Culture

The Yellow River culture has a parental spirit of incessantly striving and seeking innovation. The pre-Qin culture which originated from the Yellow River Basin possessed a remarkable spirit of innovation. In *Classic of Changes*, we can read "The changes of heaven and earth make four seasons" and "In obedience of heaven and in response to human beings, the timing of reform is of great significance!" It stresses that changes are the fundamental law of all things, including heaven and earth, and human beings should adapt to the changes of the era. The Confucian classics also stress the creativity and innovation, "A new day, another new day, all days new." The fact that advanced and leading political system was formed in the Yellow River Basin 2,000 years ago has close relationship with the fact that the Yellow River culture stresses the importance of adapting to the era and actively reforming the social institution. Shang Yang, a great reformer of the pre-Qin period, wrote, "The king was made in three dynasties without necessity of having the same rites, and five overlords were made without necessity of having the same legal system." The parental origin of the Yellow River culture has a strong realistic concern and the wish to become stronger through reforms (Fig. 4-23). The rebirth of the Yellow River culture today is in more need of inheriting the creative spirit of making changes with time passing, and striving to create the cultural system and concepts of value that are positive and enterprising and applicable to the world.

时移世易的创新精神，努力创造出积极有为、适用于世界的文化体系和价值观。

4. 包容：展现黄河文化的敦厚本质

黄河文化起源自农耕文明，体现出注重和谐、讲究秩序的敦厚稳重风格（图4-24），具有现实理性的世俗主义倾向，官僚政治发达而神权迷信色彩淡薄，对不同种族、文化接纳度高，排他性不强，故而能够包容、同化周边民族和文化，为中华民族的不断发展壮大，物质、精神文明的持续发展提供了坚实稳定的基础。在历史进程中，中国的政权虽然不断更迭，周边少数民族亦多次入主中原，但黄河文化强大的同化、包容能力，使得以其为主体的中华文化持续扩展，延续不绝。当今在世界多元化格局下，我们要重塑面向世界的黄河文化，必须更加注重黄河文化的包容性，讲究和谐共生。

图4-24 质朴厚重的黄河农业文明象征：黄土高原
Fig. 4-24 Loess Plateau, symbol of the Yellow River agricultural civilization

青海的黄河支流 摄影/ 董保华
Tributaries of the Yellow River in Qinghai Province (photo by Dong Baohua)

5. 开放：拓展黄河文化的格局气象

汉唐时期黄河文化光芒四射，辐射周边，造就中国历史上鼎盛的黄金时代，与当时社会外向开放的精神风貌有密切的关系。上层阶级积极进取，不断拓展外交边界；下层民风刚劲尚质，崇尚勇毅事功的外向性格。而明清以来黄河文化的衰落，与主政策略转向闭关锁国，自大排外，文化风气内敛保守、僵化凝固有明显的关联。对外开放，是当今黄河文化新生的必由之路（图4-25）。新时期中国立足本国又面向世界的当代中国文化"走出去"战略，为古老的黄河文化注入新的活力，呈现出积极开放的盛大格局。

图4-25　汇入大洋、面向世界：黄河出海口（山东省东营市）

Fig. 4-25　Estuary of the Yellow River: flowing into the ocean and embracing the world (Dongying City, Shandong Province)

4. Inclusiveness: Demonstration of the Profoundness of the Yellow River Culture

The Yellow River culture originated from the agricultural civilization, and demonstrated its serious and profound characteristics that stressed harmony and order (Fig. 4-24). It has a realistically rational secular tendency, and its bureaucratic politics is advanced whereas its theological power and superstition are less, and it has a high degree of acceptance of the different ethnic groups and cultures, so it can encompass and assimilate the surrounding nationalities and cultures to provide a solid foundation for the Chinese nationality to continuously develop and grow with the material and spiritual civilization's continuing development. In China's long history, political power has been constantly shifting, and the surrounding minorities have dominated the Central Plains for many times, but Chinese culture, with the Yellow River culture being the main body, continuously develops without interruption by means of the Yellow River culture's strong capability of absorption and integration. In contemporary world of diversity, when we reshape the world-oriented Yellow River culture, we must pay more attention to the inclusiveness of the Yellow River culture and stress harmonious coexistence.

5. Openness: Extension of the Setup of the Yellow River Culture

The Yellow River culture in the Han and Tang dynasties was so impressive that it influenced the surrounding countries, and helped to create a golden age in the history of China, which was closely related to the contemporary spiritual atmosphere of being open and conversant. The upper classes actively strove to broaden diplomatic boundaries, whereas the lower classes cultivated an extrovert character of resilience and bravery. The decline of the Yellow River culture since the Ming and Qing dynasties had a strong relationship with the adoption of the policy of avoiding having contacts with other countries and the strong sense of self-esteem. Opening up to the world is the necessary road to the contemporary revival of the Yellow River culture (Fig. 4-25). The contemporary "going out" strategy of Chinese culture which is based on local tradition but oriented towards the world is infusing the old Yellow River culture with new vigor to take on the grand pattern of activeness and openness.

附录：中国历史年代简表

Appendix: A Brief Chronology of Chinese History

中国历史年代简表

A Brief Chronology of Chinese History

五帝时代 Period of the Five Legendary Rulers c. 2600 BC–c. 2070 BC	黄帝 Huangdi (Yellow Emperor)	
	颛顼 Zhuanxu	
	帝喾 Diku (Emperor Ku)	
	尧 Yao	
	舜 Shun	
夏 Xia Dynasty	c. 2070 BC–c. 1600 BC	
商 Shang Dynasty	c. 1600 BC–c. 1046 BC	
西周 Western Zhou Dynasty	c. 1046 BC–c. 771 BC	
东周 Eastern Zhou Dynasty 770 BC–256 BC	春秋 Spring and Autumn Period	770 BC–476 BC
	战国 Warring States Period	475 BC–221 BC
秦 Qin Dynasty	221 BC–206 BC	
汉 Han Dynasty 206 BC–220 AD	西汉 Western Han	206 BC–25 AD
	东汉 Eastern Han	25 AD–220 AD
三国 Three Kingdoms 220 AD–280 AD	魏 Wei	220 AD–265 AD
	蜀汉 Shu Han	221 AD–263 AD
	吴 Wu	222 AD–280 AD
晋 Jin Dynasty 265 AD–420 AD	西晋 Western Jin	265 AD–317 AD
	东晋 Eastern Jin	317 AD–420 AD

Appendix: A Brief Chronology of Chinese History

续表 Continued Table

南北朝 Southern and Northern Dynasties 420 AD-589 AD	南朝 Southern Dynasties	宋 Song	420 AD-479 AD
		齐 Qi	479 AD-502 AD
		梁 Liang	502 AD-557 AD
		陈 Chen	557 AD-589 AD
	北朝 Northern Dynasties	北魏 Northern Wei	386 AD-534 AD
		东魏 Eastern Wei	534 AD-550 AD
		北齐 Northern Qi	550 AD-577 AD
		西魏 Western Wei	535 AD-556 AD
		北周 Northern Zhou	557 AD-581 AD
隋 Sui Dynasty			581 AD-618 AD
唐 Tang Dynasty			618 AD-907 AD
五代十国 Five Dynasties and Ten States	五代 Five Dynasties 907 AD-960 AD	后梁 Later Liang	907 AD-923 AD
		后唐 Later Tang	923 AD-936 AD
		后晋 Later Jin	936 AD-947 AD
		后汉 Later Han	947 AD-950 AD
		后周 Later Zhou	951 AD-960 AD
	十国 Ten States 902 AD-979 AD	北汉 Northern Han	951 AD-979 AD
		吴 Wu	902 AD-937 AD
		吴越 Wuyue	907 AD-978 AD
		闽 Min	909 AD-945 AD
		南汉 Southern Han	917 AD-971 AD
		荆南（又称"南平"） Jingnan (Nanping)	924 AD-963 AD
		楚 Chu	927 AD-951 AD
		南唐 Southern Tang	937 AD-975 AD
		前蜀 Former Shu	907 AD-925 AD
		后蜀 Later Shu	934 AD-965 AD

续表 Continued Table

宋 Song Dynasty 960 AD-1279 AD	北宋 Northern Song	960 AD-1127 AD
	南宋 Southern Song	1127 AD-1279 AD
辽 Liao (契丹 Qidan/Khitan)	907 AD-1125 AD	
西夏 Xixia (Tangut)	1038 AD-1227 AD	
金 Jin	1115 AD-1234 AD	
元 Yuan Dynasty	1206 AD-1368 AD	
明 Ming Dynasty	1368 AD-1644 AD	
清 Qing Dynasty	1616 AD-1911 AD	
中华民国 Republic of China	1912 AD-1949 AD	
中华人民共和国 People's Republic of China	1949 AD-